learning to be mothers t

to be

Fiona Lee

learning to be mothers to be mothers learning mothers learning to be

A creative, compassionate and empowering response to mothers' learning

LAP LAMBERT Academic Publishing

Impressum/Imprint (nur für Deutschland/only for Germany)
Bibliografische Information der Deutschen Nationalbibliothek: Die Deutsche Nationalbibliothek verzeichnet diese Publikation in der Deutschen Nationalbibliografie; detaillierte bibliografische Daten sind im Internet über http://dnb.d-nb.de abrufbar.

Coverbild: www.ingimage.com

Verlag: LAP LAMBERT Academic Publishing GmbH & Co. KG
Heinrich-Böcking-Str. 6-8, 66121 Saarbrücken, Deutschland
Telefon +49 681 3720-310, Telefax +49 681 3720-3109
Email: info@lap-publishing.com

Approved by: Vancouver, University of British Columbia, MA, 2010

Herstellung in Deutschland:
Schaltungsdienst Lange o.H.G., Berlin
Books on Demand GmbH, Norderstedt
Reha GmbH, Saarbrücken
Amazon Distribution GmbH, Leipzig
ISBN: 978-3-8465-4313-9

Imprint (only for USA, GB)
Bibliographic information published by the Deutsche Nationalbibliothek: The Deutsche Nationalbibliothek lists this publication in the Deutsche Nationalbibliografie; detailed bibliographic data are available in the Internet at http://dnb.d-nb.de.

Cover image: www.ingimage.com

Publisher: LAP LAMBERT Academic Publishing GmbH & Co. KG
Heinrich-Böcking-Str. 6-8, 66121 Saarbrücken, Germany
Phone +49 681 3720-310, Fax +49 681 3720-3109
Email: info@lap-publishing.com

Printed in the U.S.A.
Printed in the U.K. by (see last page)
ISBN: 978-3-8465-4313-9

Abstract

Adult learning is "a multidimensional phenomenon ... that takes place in various contexts", including those that are concurrently individual, familial, and societal (Merriam 2008, p. 97). Through a process that is located, dynamic, informal and formal, and occurs in both public and private contexts, this thesis employs autobiographical bricolage to articulate my mother learning in a rich, layered exploration and expression of insights.

Over the course of my writings, I explored my identity, role, and practices within the contexts of family relationships, communities of peers and mentors, and the wider North American context. Through this method, I articulate the spectrum of mental, emotional, psychological, relational, spiritual, embodied, and artistic learning in which I have been engaged, while also locating my self in the context of the broader educational and interdisciplinary discussions on mothering and learning.

This thesis gives shape to my mother learning journey: a process of identification and reflection which grants me insight into other parents' ways of "knowing, learning, and being" and has fostered in me the desire to facilitate and provide compassionate support for other parent learners (Grumet 1988, p. 149; Holman-Jones 2008, p. 209; Geertz 2003, p. 149). This desire to develop "a shared consciousness" is rooted in a desire to foster the "surprising insights" that Davis, et al. (2000) claim will inspire learners to continue seeking growth and challenge (Clarke & Collins 2007, p. 167; p. 148).

Self-exploration informs my role as a parent educator seeking to enrich the mutual learning of parent-learners and educators. Through clarification of the mother learning of my predecessors and by offering new "methods and meaning", I hope to incite change through a process which layers cycles of reflection and re-imagining (Byrne-Armstrong 2001, p. 72; Grumet 1988, p. 90, 93, 19; Holman-Jones 2003, p. 111).

My own transformation from an isolated, fearful, and discouraged woman who felt constrained by her mother role, to that of a layered, humbled, questioning, and resourceful mother, daughter, wife, and educator define the borders of this thesis, but not of my learning journey as a mother and parent educator. This journey continues still now.

Table of Contents

List of Figures

Acknowledgements

I want to thank a multitude of people for their love, support and encouragement during my mother-learning process and the writing of this thesis.

Thank you,
- Bobby for being there in body, mind and spirit and for, together with Naia and Anica, teaching me to love with, not in spite of, my imperfections;
- Mom for listening to what is on my mind and in my heart and soul and who, together with Christina, assists me to integrate my learning so that I might write and live out of the conviction that we are all worthy of God's love;
- Dad for responding to my crises of self-knowledge and self-confidence with empathy and encouragement;
- George and Doree for being present and loving in word and deed;
- Shauna for helping me to clarify my vision, my knowing, and my work, through patience, encouragement, advice, and presence;
- Carl for affirming the poet in me and clarifying the valuable contribution that a voice guided by faith has in the academic dialogue;
- Mona for challenging me to focus my passion and to clarify my voice;
- Jules, whose mentorship, alongside of me and from afar, has affirmed and encouraged me to be a better mother and educator;
- Dopé, my mother-partner, without whom this might not have been written; and,
- the community of Grandview Calvary Baptist Church for providing me with a spiritual home and family that reminds me that God, in Christ, loves me and that I am invited to love compassionately and actively in response.

Preface: To the Reader ...

> Whatever I do write, it is my story I am telling, my version of the past. If [another] were to tell [their] own story other landscapes would be revealed. (Rich 1986, p. 221)

My goal for this thesis is to present my stories as alternatives to the dominant discourse—a process that involves "description, not prescription" (Stadlen, 2004 p. 10). In writing my stories of mother learning I highlight the role that a number of particular people have played in my learning process.[1] However, I am not writing their stories, for they might articulate them very differently. Instead, I am describing how and when our stories intertwine and how they are complicated and enriched by these encounters. This research has received ethics approval (reference number H09-02144) from the University of British Columbia Behavioural Research Ethics Board (see Appendix 1 for more details).

As a reader, you are invited to tease apart my stories, identifying the differences from, and similarities with, your own experiences while reflecting upon and discerning the significance of what you notice. By encouraging other parents to view parenting as parent educator Naomi Stadlen (2004) does, I am affirming an approach that attempts to temper the effect of external discourses through the use of "patience, compassion, and generosity" as its primary tenets (p. 31). In so doing, I am encouraging attention to the moments and processes of parenting rather than the results.

Caveats

Here I note that memory can be a collection of "slippery" and changeable impressions (Byrne-Armstrong 2001, p. 72). My hope is that I have explored my mother-learning process with integrity, honesty, and accountability by claiming my position as a "first order" theorist and engaging those without whom none of this would be possible: the watchful eyes and ears of my family and friends; the advice, research, and reference of trusted scholars; and, the compassion of the reader (Stanley 1990, as referenced in Byrne-Armstrong 2001, p. 71).

---

[1] These include: my husband, Bobby; my children, Naia and Anica; my parents; my maternal grandparents; my godparents; and our family's nanny, Dopé.

Introduction

This thesis explores *mother learning*, specifically my own learning to be a mother and a parent educator. In using description, metaphor, and argument I demonstrate that mother learning is a significant element of lifelong learning, albeit one that has received only limited attention. Through a combination of personal narrative, poetry, and academic analysis I reveal the character and dimension of my mother-learning process, while also identifying and questioning the forces which undermined my understanding of my mother identity, role, and practice. Thus I re-invest mother learning with complexity, mystery and spirit in the context of the home, the classroom, and society at large.

Problem

Sharan Merriam (2008) describes adult learning as "a multidimensional phenomenon ... that takes place in various contexts", including those that are concurrently personal and relational, private and public, as well as individual, familial, and societal (p. 97). The process of learning to mother my two daughters triggered many doubts and questions in me about the validity of traditional sources of mother-knowledge such as health professionals and healthy baby and mothering textbooks. Adapting to the radical shift in mindset and priorities that I experienced when I transitioned from working professional to novice mother, I felt isolated, judged, and confused by the medical caregivers and educators whom I sought out for information and reassurance.

Over time many of their claims of authority weakened when compared to the mother-knowledge that I gathered during my first years of mothering. Their didactic, medical advice that centred on mothering techniques was inconsistent and lacked the wisdom, engagement, and encouragement necessary for me to grow and invest in mothering over the long term (Dobson 1983; Sears & Sears 2001; Murkoff, Eisenburg, & Hathaway 2003). The main challenge for me is not how to *do for* my children, but how to *be with* them; my desire is not to attend only to the mundane tasks of feeding, clothing, and shuttling them here and there rather to learn how to connect with them through honest, reflective and loving initiative and response over a lifetime of mothering. Consequently, I have spent my mothering career investigating, abandoning, and

3

adapting various types of knowledge and practice, while discovering more creative alternatives on which to draw.

Mothering & Epistemology

The parenting discourses that I, a new parent, encountered in books and in practice recommended the expert medical professional as the logical resource for the uncertain, the *impaired*, and therefore incapable parent (Leach 1997; Dobson 1985; Murkoff et al. 2003). These discourses emphasize the value of a clinician's emotional distance from the intimate personal relationships between a mother and her child, rather than recognizing the unique insights that each mother possesses. This diminishment of mother knowledge often caused me to be critical of myself rather than question the vague and hierarchical nature of this epistemological system.

Upon the birth of my first daughter, I tentatively questioned my medical caregivers, but my doubts were regularly dismissed. My specific, embodied, relational, and spiritual knowledge of my child could not compete with their rational knowledge of studies and statistics (Code 1991, p. 6; Fenwick 2003a, p. 124; Burrell 1988, p. 224; Tisdell 2008, p. 33) (see Figure 1).

In frustration I sought out other resources, only to find that the majority of well-known parenting literature did not question dominant modes of knowing as exemplified by educated, Caucasian, heterosexual, male, medical experts (Spock & Needleman 2004; Sears & Sears 2001; Ehrenreich & English 2005). Despite being white, heterosexual, well educated, middle class, and English-speaking I began to understand how capricious society was in having particular knowledge deemed necessary by an elite group of power brokers (Dewey 1934, p. 43; Fenwick 2003, p.126). My protests were silenced by the Cartesian discourse that denies its own partiality and determines not only "what can be said and thought, but also who can speak, when, and with what authority" (Ball 1990, p. 2; Foucault 1984, p. 56).

Figure 1: Sources of Mother Knowledge
(based on Horowitz & Long 2005, pp.100-103)

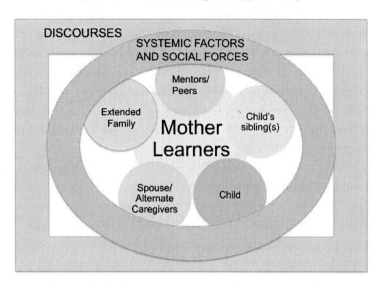

My insecurities were compounded by my subsequent diagnosis of postpartum anxiety disorder (a form of postpartum depression). Doubting my physical capability, psychological consistency, and spiritual conviction, I questioned whether I would ever become a worthy mother (Dunlop 1998, p. 107; Middleton, 2005 p. 2; Laino, 2008 p. 16; Pruett, 2000, p. 197; Levy 2000, p. 86). My gender, my depression, and my lack of medical qualifications labeled me as an inferior participant in this discussion (Code 1991, p. 223; Smith 1987, p. 83-84,154; Grumet 1988, pp. xvi-xvii; Lakoff & Johnson 1999, p. 17; Ehrenreich & English 2005, p. 113).

Struggling to maintain both my private and public self, I did not know how to reconcile my mother-self with my other life roles of daughter, friend, sister, and wife, let alone that of articulate critical thinker and professional educator (Grumet 1988, p. 165; Levy 2000, p. 86). It took years before I began to trust the value of my own embodied, relational, and creative abilities for learning and even more before I understood the value of sharing my insights with others.

Embodiment, Relationship & Spirituality

Mothering two daughters has taught me that self-knowledge is embodied, relational and spiritual. We learn through: a) how we interact bodily with others both in proximity and in touch, b) listening to our bodily limitations and being stretched by our strength and stamina, and c) inquiring as to both the depth and the superficiality of body image and awareness. By investigating who has the power to assess and determine the validity of body knowledge, I am not only questioning my understanding of mother learning, but also interrogating the "privilege" and "regulation" which frame our values and define our practices (Burrell 1988, p. 224; Hartnett and Engels 2008, p. 588; Kincheloe & Berry 2004, p. 7).

This is no simple endeavour (Chandler 1998, p. 284). Since individuals, couples, and entire family networks span cultures, languages, geography, politics, ages, genders, religions, and sexualities, there is no one view of embodied parent learning. Thus the knowledge each learner gains must be considered in relation to these elements and be regarded as partial and located rather than explicit, comprehensive, timeless, and replicable (Holman-Jones 2008, p. 209; Overton 2004, p. 31). This multiplicity of learners and knowledge does not inhibit learning but rather results in more resonant and profound knowledge for learners who strive to be adaptable, creative, and participatory, rather than simply rational and goal-oriented (Davis, Sumara & Kapler 2000, pp. 144, 147; Karpiak 2000a, p. 35; Dunlop 1998, p. 121; Tisdell 2008, p. 33).

Due to our "interdependence" our understanding of ourselves as discrete learners is blurred by our relationships with our partners, our parents, our siblings, and our children (Chandler 1998, p. 274; Dunlop 1998, p. 106) (see Figure 3). Through relational strengthening, communal "acknowledgement, correction, and critique", as well as self-exploration, reconciliation, and integration, our bodies, minds, souls, practice, and relationships all serve as means of creative self-expression and learning (Dunlop 1998, p. 108; Tisdell 2008, p. 32-33; Karpiak 2005, p. 96; Springgay 2004, p. 42-43; Rich 2001, p. 8, 11; Code 1991, p. 224).

Figure 2: The Complexity of the Learning Process
(Adapted from Varela, Thompson & Rosch 199, pp. 10-11)

'What is learned is always a complex matter of historical circumstance, immediate context, and anticipated activity' (Davis, et al. 2000, p. 144)

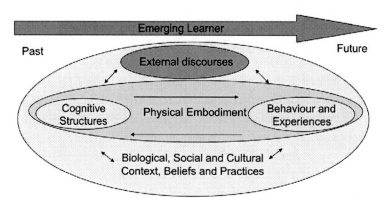

Research Questions:

The epistemological, embodied, relational, and spiritual character of mother learning, touched upon briefly here, are explored in more depth in the body of this thesis. The key questions guiding these explorations are:

What is mother learning?

What types of knowledge have fostered my mother learning?

In what ways do different discourses about mother learning and sources of mother knowledge silence or delegitimize mother learning?

How did my research into *Empowered Mothering* writings encourage me to voice my own mother learning process and insights?

How has my autobiographical inquiry shaped my own identity and informed my practice as a parent educator?

What recommendations for parent education can be made based on this autobiographical inquiry into my own mother learning?

Mother Learning

Mothering is not entirely instinctual (Ehrenreich & English 2005, p. 243). There are no naturally born mothers who innately know all there is to know about being a mother. Likewise, a vast sum of experience will not afford complete understanding of motherhood. It is not possible to determine definitively the foremost authority on mother-knowledge. Regardless of whether one has twenty children or none, there will forever remain elements of mystery to being a mother (Stadlen 2004, p. 103).

Mothering is not a replicable science. Mothers cannot go to school or train to become the kind of *expert* who will possess all of the answers on how to mother any child in every possible situation perfectly (Ehrenreich & English 2005, p. 251). While mother learners cannot develop an exhaustive knowledge base about mothering, neither can they perfect their expertise in "techniques" and "training" (Maté and Neufeld 2005: 51-52; Shorthouse 2009-2010: 28). Yet mother learners can still learn about their role, identity and practice.

Dislocation from both immediate and extended family networks has made the traditional apprenticeship models of mother learning a physical impossibility and resulted in a learning vacuum for those of us preparing to have, and having, children (Man 2001 p. 428). Within this vacuum, numerous so-called 'experts' from a variety of disciplines have emerged and have claimed to possess ultimate knowledge of *best* parenting practices (Dobson 1983; Sears & Sears 2001; Murkoff, et al. 2003; Leach 1997; Ehrenreich & English 2005; Nathanson & Tuley 2008). Rather than affirming and fostering discussions about a diversity of parent/child relationships, these experts have identified a narrow category of familial relationships as valid models of *mothering*, *fathering*, and *families*.

Some parenting discourses discount the "intensity" of mothering, the emotional, psychological, physical, and spiritual investment required to mother (Stadlen 2004, p. 14-15). Instead, bearing a child and adjusting to being a mother is seen as a minor interruption, after which women will be able to return to the regular rhythm of their lives (p. 33). In particular, these external discourses have a tendency to blame the individual for their circumstances and over simplify the causes and responsibility for managing stressful circumstances rather than granting insight into their complexity (Horwitz &

8

Long 2005, pp. 102-103).

Unlike Maté and Neufeld (2005), whose book *Hold onto your kids: Why parents need to matter more than peers* has become a touchstone for parents wanting to remain integral to their children's lives as they grow, I do not claim to be an "authority" who can "teach what is most fundamental to effective parenting" (cover description; p. 50). Rather, I use my own life as an example of how I discerned over time and through my family relationships what mattered most to me as a mother: that my children knew that Bobby, their father, and I loved them. Through my autobiographical writings and teaching practices I am seeking to identify the types of, and contexts for, mother, and father, learning while demonstrating the need to model compassion for the hope and the costs that define this process of gathering knowledge.

Starting out as a parent educator and advocate I lacked the confidence in myself so I sought to gain external affirmation for my personal knowledge and experience. As a result I chose to pursue certification as a postnatal educator to validate my own learning. While acquiring my training hours I worked alongside a variety of mother nad father learners whose knowledge and experience reaffirmed my previous belief that *mother learning is not comprised of a cohesive block of fixed, absolute certainties and does not require expert guidance to be refined and claimed.* Since mother and father learners are in relationship with one or more unique children, guided by chosen mentors, and in dialogue with a select community of fellow learners, their learning is a loose collection of personal, temporal, geographic, lived experiences and reflection as perceived by particular learners which is dynamic and changing in relevance and value.

This multiplicity of learners, perspectives and knowledge does not inhibit learning but rather garners more resonant and profound insights through critical decision-making and introspective discussion (see Figure 3). Mother, and father, learners can employ these essential tools throughout this fluid process by reflecting upon their previous experience, evaluating their current priorities and envisioning future interactions. By engaging with their fellow learners in honest and open deliberation and dialogue, mothers and fathers can discern valuable lessons, gain new understanding or apply previously unfamiliar parenting principles (Foucault 1984, p. 24-25; Kincheloe & Berry 2004, p. 3; Aston 2002, p. 287-288; Capra 1984, p. 6).

9

Figure 3: Situational Awareness in Dynamic Decision-Making
(Adapted from Endsley 1995, p. 34)

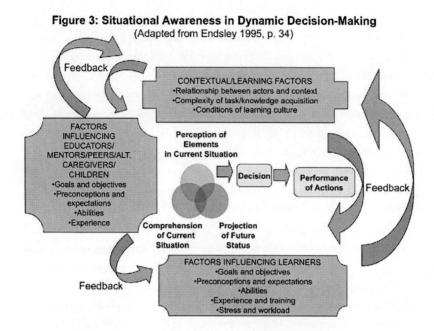

While mothering two daughters, studying adult learning, and training as a postnatal educator, I am engaging in this learning dialogue with my fellow mother and father learners, their experience, their questions, their insights, their struggles, and their investments through my listening, reading, writing, speaking, and acting.

In this context I am careful to assert that while I am a mother learner engaged in a continuous and intensive study of mother learning, not a day passes that I am not tempted to claim an epiphany that might lead me to becoming the undisputed authority on mother-wisdom. However, on most occasions I choose to occupy the shifting sands of the learning process, and resolve to persevere in offering compassion and humility, rather than judgment.

This living in the space in-between my blissful ideal, societal expectations and the failure I fear lies just around the corner, gives mother learning its complexity (Ehrenreich & English 2005, p. 357-358). By exploring and articulating my own learning honestly I can imagine and enact creative learning possibilities while seeking to claim integrity in this challenging process (Dickau 2010a, afterword; Karpiak 2005, p. 97, 100, 102).

> To seek visions, to dream dreams, is essential, and it is also essential to try new ways of living, to make room for serious experimentation, to respect the effort even where it fails. (Rich 1986, p. 282)

Method

> The mother is myth, metaphor, memory, and real flesh and blood—a
> fascinating and pervasive topic of poetry. (Dunlop 2007, p. 2)

Bricolage

I implore you as poet and mother
keep the edges unfinished,
ragged and uneven.

Suppress the desire
to tie off all the threads
for we do not know the outcome
nor achieve full satisfaction
if the picture
is neatly squared away.

Through my learning and writing, with Pinar I seek "subjectivity as a passage to, rather than a retreat from, the world" (in press, p. 11). By exploring and articulating my own learning both honestly and imaginatively, I can form suggestions for alternative learning possibilities for myself and other mother learners (Karpiak 2005, p. 97, 100, 102).

The Shape of My Thesis

I employ autobiographical bricolage to reveal the many socio-cultural conceptions of mothering and learning. These have served both to obstruct and to further my understanding of and commitment to investing in my mothering role and practices. Autobiography is considered to be both a literary recording of life experience and a process of identifying the ways in which the self is constructed in the socio-cultural context and by beliefs and priorities (Eakin 1999; Grumet 1987; Butler & Bentley 1996) (see Figure 1). I seek to include both aspects of autobiography in my thesis by incorporating multiple styles of writing to express my embodied vulnerabilities, relational investments, spiritual story, professional aspirations, and my journey of learning.

In order to articulate the richness of the mother-learning process, I explore my own path of gathering mother-knowledge by "weaving intricate connections among life and art, experience and theory, evocation and explanation" integrating poetry, narrative, and academic writings on mother learning (Holman-Jones 2008, p. 208). Together with personal narratives that include daily teaching and learning, I layer autobiographical, poetic reflections of and possibilities for my mother-learning process alongside analytical consideration of the discourses that have influenced me. Called bricolage, this method of "thick description" facilitates my examination of the dynamics involved in seeking knowledge by claiming what is valid or, conversely, identifying weaknesses in the dominant discourse (Kincheloe & Berry 2004, p. 16) (See Figure 3).

This storying, retelling, and re-imagining shifts my autobiographical accounts of learning from "dogmatism" to wondering, from instruction to conversation (Grumet 1997, pp. 324-325). Locating, mediating, questioning, and listening sustains the dialogue between my personal writing and teaching and the contributions of my fellow mother-learners, parent educators, and academic scholars while it tests my limits and knowledge (Kenyon & Randall 1997; Mezirow 1990; Byrne-Armstrong 2001; Karpiak 2000b & 2005; Butt & Raymond 1989; Rossiter 2002).

With time I have discerned that mothering requires me to pause, to retreat, to re-examine, and to re-articulate that which puzzles me, which defeats me, and which I am seeking to overcome (Grumet 1988, p. 86, 88). This can be like a dance with many partners: flowing beautifully at times, the intentions and actions of the various elements synchronized, while at other times, the dissonance is almost catastrophic (Clarke & Collins, 2007 p. 164). As I fumble along, day-to-day, employing my individual gifts and making allowances for my various mis-steps, I am continually constructing "poetic" explanations of my learning, by presenting my learning and practice to those with whom I learn (Freeman 2007, p. 136; Smith 1987, p. 9).

In my autobiographical narrative, poetry, and letter writing, as well as my critical research and teaching I illuminate what is unseen and unspoken in the dominant discourse by learning "*with*, *in*, and *through*" my mothering practice and the parent learning processes of others (Springgay, Irwin & Wilson Kind 2005, p. 899). This dynamic process of inquiry is called a/r/tography. I engage in the world at large through my critical, creative, and theoretical dialogue with other learners and educators by deciphering, crafting, and interpreting text, knowledge, and meaning (Sinner, Leggo, Irwin, Gouzzouasis & Grauer 2006, p. 1224). As an educator I create the context for discussion, for creative conjecture that informs and inspires, which in turn is informed and inspired by the practice in which the learners are engaged.

As I wrestle with the tensions between my experience, my expression, and my understanding of the mother learning and knowing process, I scrutinize, probe, and reveal *what parenting is, what it is not*, and *what it could be* (Springgay, Irwin & Wilson Kind 2005, p. 905, 908). If I can listen for, as well as question, imaginative ideas in my life I can elevate myself, my mothering, my writing and my teaching to new "possibilities" (Soyini-Madison 2003, p. 476; Geertz 2003, p. 147; Holman-Jones 2003, p. 108).

By mothering without pretense I hope to provide a refreshing perspective to fellow mother and father learners seeking to thrive amidst the ups and downs of family life. I argue that mother and father learning are complex yet hopeful processes that can empower us to seek and identify legitimate emerging alternatives, rather than prescribe new formulae for parenting. In so doing I am claiming and creating new knowledge as it claims and creates me as a mother learner and knower (Springgay, Irwin & Wilson Kind 2005, p. 899). At the same time, I am suggesting alternative knowers and knowledge: mother and father learners, our children, our peers, and our mentors who together foster a dialogue redefined by humility, inclusion, and possibility as we re-envision and reinvest in lived inquiry (p. 906).

Autobiography as Method: What Can Stories Teach Us?

> I struggle with the possibilities of storytelling, of recounting my narratives in a world of work in which academic discourse traditionally excludes close scrutiny of our personal lives as work of intellectual merit ... our personal narratives of reading and writing the body might be perceived as indiscretion, telling too much, signs of inadequacy in the lack of separation of public and private experiences. (Dunlop 1998, p. 119)

Following an undergraduate education that told me that "I" was not a subject of legitimate academic research, I struggled to find a subject and a style of writing for my Masters degree that would articulate the range of my experience. Experiences of mothering that included doubting, despairing, questioning, loving, stretching, hoping, and learning were largely lacking from the discourse of parent education that I had unearthed. As time passed, I began to grasp that I must listen to and learn from myself: my body, my psyche, my faith, and my sentiments. Slowly I began to trust that these insights could be shared with others so that they might be spared a measure of the self-doubt and frustration that I had experienced (Karpiak 2005, p. 96).

Even as I began to research and write about mother learning, I did not find affirmation for first-hand anecdotes for formal educational purposes. However, as I began to reflect upon which methods of parent education have most influenced me I realized how stories have framed, modeled, and fostered much of the learning which has been significant in my own life: the Biblical narrative that has given context to my lifelong faith journey; the vivid accounts of trial and error, humility and welcome of my family and community members; and the varied descriptions of mother learning (and father learning) which convinced me that I was not alone in my struggles to adapt to mothering.

When I reviewed the parenting volumes which I continually reference and recommend, I realized that they comprised two major types of biographical writing: autobiographical stories which recount mother and/or father learning, and edited works containing case studies and/or biographical accounts of mother and/or father identity and adaptation issues (Aron, 2002; Sheedy Kurcinka 1998; Stadlen 2004; Sandborn 2007; Pruett 2001; Howard 2007; Iovine 2007; Limbo & Rich Wheeler 1986; Pacific Postpartum Support Society 2002; Johnson & Solem 2007; Farber & Mazlish 2004; Nelson, et al. 2007).

I come from a long line of worriers: some were claustrophobic, others depressed, and still others suffered from anxiety that ate away at them relentlessly. Unfortunately, little of these personal details were openly discussed in my family, so when I was diagnosed with post-partum depression, manifesting as anxiety disorder, it was a nasty shock to me.

Following my elder daughter's birth, I immediately felt that I was expected to attend and adapt to multiple, diverse, and dynamic variables which themselves have layers of complexity and unpredictability (Fenwick 2003b, p. 9). Under the weight of these perceived expectations, mothering Naia felt like an overwhelming responsibility.

My family history, combined with a very vocally unhappy infant, and the lack of a network of extended family and friends outside of the job that I had precipitously left due to pregnancy complications put me in a very vulnerable position (ICEA 2003, p. 3).

15

Reluctant to unburden myself to others for fear of criticism or dismissal, I isolated myself, exacerbating my circumstances rather than relieving them (Laino 2008, p. 16; Pruett 2000, p. 197).

Like other parents, both mothers and fathers, whose infants were "more difficult, less adaptable, and more unpredictable", I did not discern that the multiple stressors in my life and the external discourses on mothering and stress were contributing to my self-loathing while I was merely "coping" (ICEA 2003, p. 3; Horowitz & Long 2005, p. 100, 102; Grumet 1987, p. 322). In particular, these external discourses have a tendency to blame the individual for their circumstances and over simplify the causes and responsibility for managing stressful circumstances rather than granting insight into their complexity (Horowitz & Long 2005, pp. 102-103).

Thankfully, a wise friend advised me to stop blaming myself and trying to *fix* what I perceived was *wrong* with Naia, but instead to try and *accept* us both for *who we are*. This truly was a revolutionary idea for me—to simply *be a mother learning*. Since then I have worked to resist the impulse to *do*, to *provide*, to *perfect*, to *make things happen*, when simply *being* or *learning* seem the wiser options.

The first resource which I came upon which affirmed this approach was called: *Raising your spirited child: A guide for parents whose child is more intense, sensitive, perceptive, persistent, energetic.* In this book, Mary Sheedy Kurcinka (1998) writes of her desire to find a community of parents who would support her in affirming the gifts her son possessed, rather than only seeing his "weaknesses" (p. 9). For the first time, I recognized a fellow mother who didn't ignore the dissonance between her own desires and the public discourses on parenting, but sought to question those expectations and provide an alternate understanding of how to learn, to live, and to be.

I propose that mothering and fathering are not "competitions" through which we seek to raise the healthiest, smartest, and most successful children (Daly 2004, p. 8). As a result, I have sought to shift the foci of my mothering and my parent education away from an orientation of "hyper-parenting" (p. 11). Instead I approach both mothering and educating others as "humbling" endeavours that I will never master (Stadlen 2004, p. 4). At the same time, I try to foster wisdom, "compassion", and understanding among other mother and father learners (p. 256).

By speaking clearly and directly to both mother and father learners about my ambiguous sense of authority and revealing my fragility through sharing my ambivalent feelings about my role and practice, I hope that I might develop a trust between us. Rooted in my willingness to listen to both their strengths and weaknesses, to offer them encouragement, and to empower them to fully embrace their roles as mother and father learners I am a more authentic learner and educator (Sheedy Kurcinka 1998; Stadlen 2004; Sandborn 2007; Pruett 2001; Howard 2007; Iovine 2007; Pacific Postpartum Support Society 2002; Grumet 1987, pp. 319, 323). This enmeshing of living, learning, and meaning-making both complicates my knowing and enriches my learning by connecting me to others through the generation of parent knowledge. As we resist and refine, stretch and expand our understanding of parenting and parent learning, we are claiming our knowledge and our status as knowledge generators and cultivating the learning dialogue at the same time.

Prologue: Saturday, October 20th, 2007 12:46 am

Naia and Anica,

I have so much to say, but where to start ... for some time now I have lacked confidence in myself and in my ability to articulate so many of the disparate thoughts and feelings about mothering which I have had. Therefore, I hope that in this letter, and in whatever reflections are to follow, I will help you to recognize who I am and differentiate me from the roles that I fulfill and perform: those of daughter, woman, wife, educator, and mother.

To give you insight into my role as your mother I will describe my transition from daughter and wife alone to that of mother as well. As you know, shortly before you were born, Naia, my grandmother died and I lost my first child to miscarriage. What you may not be aware of is my belief that I could fill these voids with another child and dive headlong into motherhood. However, in so doing I risked both my fragile sense of self and my marriage to your dad. Chasing what I thought was my 'mother-destiny' doggedly blinded me both to the grief that I dared not face and to the anxieties that I bore about what lay ahead of me. I now know that I was reckless in the intensity of my focus, while

17

being vastly unprepared for the physical, emotional, psychological, and spiritual demands of motherhood.

When I was finally diagnosed with postpartum anxiety, with the help of a network of support I began to acknowledge, accept, and manage my consummate ability to second-guess my skills and undermine my instincts regarding intimate relationships. Over the course of my first year of motherhood, I was grateful to realize that my unease was rooted in my desire to be a more honest and humble parent, but that initially I lacked the direction, chemical composition, and commitment to follow through on my intentions. I now recall this restlessness being inside of me alongside of you in my womb, Naia, and in a matter of months it had grown into a palpable passion to share my feelings, experiences, and impressions with you in order to heal myself and build a stronger connection with you.

At first, I believed that I ought to record my impressions in a regular, disciplined manner, as in journaling. And yet, just as I had before when deciding to write in a diary, I felt as though I had many more essential and pressing things that required my immediate and undivided attention. In addition, I am now able to admit that I have never viewed myself as articulate or insightful enough to record my reflections for your perusal or for anyone else's. For, despite the sporadic gasps of poetry that I have written and my many goals that I am pursuing, I have never thought of myself as having achieved the status of a 'writer'.

In the interim I have sought to speak my thoughts to you, Naia and Anica, in teachable moments by giving you insight into my motivations and my choices. Yet now I feel that the time has come to commit to writing as well. Not just to provide a record of my apologies, regrets, and failed dreams but of my aspirations and prayers that can provide a critical perspective of my daily interaction with you both. At the same time, I hope that this account can fuel my passion to become a more transparent, reflective, and humble mother who is willing to learn from and with you and others.

I must risk to tell

My Story
when judged and cast aside,
I wonder if I can bear

the pain I feel and fear.

Who will be my audience,
I wonder and I dread?
I trust, no I pray, for compassion
so that I may endure ...

I am worthy
of these words and images
and the labour which brings them forth.

You are my loves,
and my occupation,
my passion,
and much more;
despite my failings, great,
you all do define me,
and this I will not change.

So when and how
do I declare my self, my voice;
abiding longing
until hope can reveal me,
your mother,
certain once more?

A Day in the Life of a Mom and Parent Educator

I woke up today, Wednesday, May 14th, at 7:10 am to a peaceful quiet, rather than the yelling or crying which usually wakes me. However, when I rolled over to try to get a few more minutes of sleep I heard Anica singing the alphabet song. It makes me grin how she sings the sounds of the song even though, at two years old, she doesn't actually know her alphabet yet.

Within 2 minutes, Naia, Anica's five year-old sister, was cuddling up to me in bed and asking me to read her a book. Once I had agreed, she released me to get Anica out of her crib so that they could each choose a book. I have to admit that I miss reading quietly in the mornings on a regular basis like Naia and I used to do before Anica became so rambunctious; I loved the snuggles and easy transition time we shared together. However, to be honest we probably wouldn't have the opportunity to do it very often anyhow since we have a limited time frame in which to get Naia ready for school in the morning.

Two minutes later, while their morning milk was warming, I was trying to sneak a moment of peace on the toilet. Apparently, however, it was not meant to be since yells of "MAMA! MAMA!" soon began descending from the upstairs. When I replied that I was warming her bottle, Anica said, "Oh, nanoo," (her version of thank you) and I realized how gratifying it was to hear her using the manners that I sometimes feel as though I am pounding into her everyday.

The next step in the daily routine is to encourage Anica to remove her diaper, sit on the potty seat and try to have a pee, before we wash her hands and change her diaper. Today she decided to begin the process by using the seat like a Frisbee. Naturally this elicited an exasperated, "Please don't throw that!" from me. Delivered as it was in a rather high-pitched voice, it might have prompted further reactionary behaviour, but instead it was closely followed by a relieved, "... okay, good job," in response to her quick retrieval and righting of the potty seat. Almost simultaneously, she sat and peed, closing with an exuberant: "Yay, Anica" for her efforts. In order to ensure that she washes her hands, my newest strategy is getting her excited about making soap bubbles after going to the bathroom. I am learning more and more ways to make the routines fun and appealing as I accumulate experience as a mom, which is like gold when dealing with kids. However, as you will learn when reading through my narrative, I am often completely drained by the amount of creativity that I expend in an average day.

Next, we moved on to a popular refrain: "If you're a monkey and you know it, your name is Anica ..." complete with various edits and actions included in order to gain cooperation during the diapering routine. Then we discussed the colours on her Dora toothbrush and whether she could wear a disposable diaper since we only had a couple of the cloth diapers remaining before the Friday routine delivery of clean ones. At that point her sister entered wearing the tights she had requested to wear that day, prompting Anica to assume that she would be matching her sister and must choose her favourite pair to wear with a skirt.

Believing them to be happily dressing I returned to my room to get on my bike clothes, but was interrupted after only donning my pants. Screams of, "NO!" and "That's not yours!" brought me racing down the hall to discover Naia and Anica in full pitched battle over a Polly Pocket, her pets, and her wardrobe contents. With a few efforts at distraction, I was able to lure Anica away so that Naia could spirit her Polly Pocket back to the safety of her room. With a sigh of relief, I returned to my own room to collect the various piles of items that needed to be taken back downstairs, making an effort to return them to their rightful places, rather than dumping them in a new pile on my counter top.

While comforting Naia over a piece of Polly Pocket's possessions that Anica had newly destroyed, my antennae pricked up as I became aware of Anica's absence from downstairs. Faintly hearing her call of "Mama", I reflected that I regularly have to suppress my desire to interrupt whatever I am doing to race off and investigate the trouble in which Anica has enmeshed herself; I especially have to remind myself to listen to Naia's frustrations by being physically and emotionally present to her in the moment, rather than abandoning her to put out the fires her sister starts. After a few minutes of attending to Naia's feelings, I put bread into the toaster oven and then calmly proceeded upstairs, searching both the first and second floors before finding Anica occupied at her dad's desk on the third floor.

After carefully extracting her from the treasure trove of adult stuff located in our shared study and carrying her back downstairs she asked me for a "man". I paused briefly and then told her that she was too young for one. However, because she wanted a pen and regularly was able to find one, she was not satisfied with my response. My use of humour did not go unnoticed by Naia, but like a teenager she raised her eyebrows and said, "What?" dismissively and turned back to the toast I had recently given her.

Thankfully I noticed the Polly Pocket on the floor before Anica did, and exclaimed to Naia, "I don't understand you, just moments ago you were complaining about your sister's treatment of your toy. Don't tempt her again by leaving it lying about where she can find it so easily!" Reluctantly she agreed to return it upstairs, but not before I could doubt whether it was fair of me to expect her to police her own toys at only 5 years old. Then I reminded myself that she usually rose to the challenge and proved herself worthy of the higher expectations, while at the same time it allowed her to maintain some of her more special toys as her own, safe from her sister's diabolical plans.

While Naia carried on a virtually incessant conversation during breakfast, interrupted only by my pleas to "eat" or "drink", I zoomed around the kitchen preparing and serving food, packing bags and organizing communications with teachers. When I paused to write a few more notes on my pad, Naia queried what I was doing, and when I explained how I was chronicling the days' interactions and my impressions of them she declared that she would "help me not to lose them" (my notes). Sometimes, it is good to have a five year-old personal assistant!

My warnings of our impending departure initially elicited bleats of anxiety from Naia before there was a sudden period of silence, which although brief, was welcome and satisfying. However, no sooner had I noted it then Naia was exclaiming, "I ate all my yoghurt and toast and drank all my milk!" With exhortations to clear her dishes and go brush her teeth, she ran upstairs while I shoveled yoghurt into Anica's mouth and noted what I had not yet gathered for the remainder of our day's plans. Since there was no time to give Naia a choice for her daily fruit and vegetable snack I grabbed 2 bananas close at hand and both girls' new steel water bottles, shoving them into their respective backpacks. I can't wait until we find out that all our efforts to avoid the carcinogens in BPA plastic has led us to drink out of even more contaminated steel containers. Yes, I know that I sound cynical, but I find our culture of guilt and fear exhausting and limitless in its intrusion into every aspect of our personal and family lives.

When Naia reappeared a bit too soon, I sought to confirm that she had brushed her teeth and was ready to head off for school; however, she looked at me blankly and I had to dog her every step to ensure she followed through on my instructions. More than anything else, I hate feeling like an enforcer during these intense morning preparations and look back fondly, if inaccurately, on the slower pace of life before my daughters started school. And yet, I know that I got very little down time with Naia at home, since she thrived on constant interaction and blossomed only when she had more adults (than just me), and kids as well, with whom she could interact, and from whom she could learn.

In order to engage Anica's cooperation I let her in on the day's agenda, including dropping Naia off at school and biking back home before going to Riley Park Library for *Storytime*. To end the morning we planned to return to the school to pick up Naia in time for her to have a play date with a friend. When Anica asked about Grammy, she made me wistful about my mom's recent visit and I was forced to tell her that Grammy wouldn't be able to join us at the library today, but reminded her that we had had lots of fun with her the last time we were there. At this she nodded happily and made ready to leave. It amazes me how with some of the things that hit me hardest, kids are able to move on so quickly!

Once we finally made it to the garage we were almost knocked flat by the aroma of the Korean pickled radish I had made the night before. If Naia had known how to swear I am sure that she would have at that moment, but instead, when she learned what the source of the smell was, she said, "... well, at least it will keep the robbers away!" At that moment, I thought that her retorts were bound to get her in trouble one day, and yet my sense of humour won out and I heartily agreed with her, despite her tendency to be a 'smartypants'.

Feeling chuffed with myself that we had made reasonable time thus far and might actually get Naia to school on time, I rallied the troops into the bike trailer and pulled all 90 plus lbs out into the vegetable mist falling from the Vancouver sky. Of course, by the time we reached the light at the end of our alleyway, we started a series of dramas that would eat away at almost all of our head start on the day. First, while waiting for the light to turn green the rain cover unhinged from its useless Velcro moorings and slapped the girls right in their faces. Trying to manhandle it back into place (well, that's a sexist turn of phrase isn't it?) meant that I almost missed the light and had to jump onto the sidewalk to avoid being mowed down by the Main Street rush hour traffic. Feeling sheepish since I am a bit of a 'die hard' about scolding other cyclists who ride on the sidewalk, I returned to the side streets for the remainder of our trip. Mercifully, we arrived at school just as Naia's class was lining up to go inside so I was able to feel as though my perseverance was worth it.

The final insult to the extra effort required for biking to and from school occurred just as we were trying to navigate the construction zone occupying the lot next to the school. A motorist almost ran Anica and me down when he ignored a stop sign. Thankfully I have had enough similar experiences to distrust all drivers, so I swerved to avoid, first his front bumper, and then the remainder of his car, as he continued apologetic, yet undeterred through the intersection, while I stopped dumbfounded in the centre of the it.

Before departing the schoolyard, Anica and I had engaged in a lengthy negotiation over whether or not she would zip up or even wear her raincoat. However, I clearly lost out in the tussle since by the time we left she was not only without her coat, but she also would not allow the trailer cover, waterproof blanket, or rain cover to provide her with protection from the elements. Passing her future preschool teacher as we left I shrugged my shoulders and said that I hoped her determination would serve the forces of good some day rather than evil! Unfortunately for the rest of the trip home I was subjected to a variety of judgmental looks and shocked gazes as we passed pedestrians, fellow cyclists, and car drivers who stared at the two of us becoming more and more drenched over the course of the 15 minute return ride home.

Having dug in her heels and been sufficiently rained on, Anica arrived home happy as a clam, if soaked to the skin. While I couldn't wait to get out of my clothes at the back door, she on the other hand, preferred trailing the mud, grass, and water from the ride and the backyard into every room in the house. One of my greatest frustrations with our home is the tiny vestibule that we have at our back door with only enough room to swing open the door without banging it into the closet door directly in front of it. Lacking any place to sit down and remove clothing or any reasonable space to store it while it dries, this entrance grates on me daily during both the wet and mud of winter and the sand and grass of summer!

Further irritations about our home surfaced as Anica and I headed upstairs to change her diaper where I spied her leaking bedroom ceiling. We are currently having roof tiles replaced, membranes repaired, downspouts fitted and extended, and new decking installed, we have yet to smoothly navigate our negotiations with either the roofing or envelope repair companies; while this process has cost us about $15,000.00

to date, it has also drained immeasurable amounts of energy and caused much anxiety and frustration. Today, in fact, we were due to receive a revised quote for our decks since the previous estimate was very slim on detail and high on cost, yet I have not had any time yet to check if it has in fact come through via email.

Despite all this, I am loathed to leave our home that is bright, airy, open, and very functional for an active foursome. I also love how we can open our doors and extend our hospitality to extended family and friends from out of town so that they can use our home as their base from which to explore the area or attend work-related events. In addition, the kids' friends can drop by for a morning or afternoon and have lots of space to play or nap as need be. Furthermore, I hope to eventually hold parent education classes or workshops out of my home, both as a means of saving on overhead and in order to overcome some of the hurdles which get in the way of sharing intimately in the context of adult education.

My sales job regarding the yoghurt which I had bought the girls as a special treat was entirely lost on Anica: since it is sweetened with fruit juice rather than just sugar, she certainly doesn't like it as much as the artificially flavoured ones she has been spoiled by in the past. Even less interesting to her, but important to me, is the fact that this yoghurt comes in recyclable containers as opposed to the throw away ones which, though eye-catching and stackable toys in the interim, must be thrown away, inducing guilt and frustration in me.

Therefore, in order to distract Anica, I grabbed the fake *fly girl* headset which Naia had received from McDonalds and let her use it while I attempted to feed her the remaining yoghurt. Despite the fact that the 3 repetitive bars of music make my head swim, Anica fixed her eyes firmly on the animal crackers which I used as an additional incentive for her to finish the yoghurt and swayed to the beat of the music.

My next dilemma was how I would entertain her sufficiently while I got my shower. When I opened the CD stand to play some of the dance music she loves, I found myself immediately discouraged on viewing the devastation that used to be our pristine pre-Anica cd collection. For all her vices as a baby, Naia never challenged the limits we placed upon her to the extent that Anica has done. Even as a toddler, Anica seems to have little if any regard for the consequences which Bobby and I have used in our attempts to stem her destructive nature. Hiding and locking up our stuff is the best way that we have found to preserve our belongings--even to the extent that I have completely lost track of some of the things that I have tried to prevent Anica from finding. Despite this tangential train of thought, I managed to find a rocking cd and left her to spin away happily in her dress-up clothes for a couple of minutes while I cleaned up.

Returning to the family room and kitchen area, I realized that although I was planning to clean up before Naia's friend was due to arrive at lunchtime we were already approaching library time. Concluding that once again my OCD desires would have to be stayed for the sake of toddler satisfaction, I made for the door with Anica firmly wedged, and giggling, under my arm!

However, as soon as I inquired whether she was ready to set off for the library, Anica informed me that she had pooed and I was required to race upstairs for an extra cloth diaper. When she followed me up to flush away her poo, I asked her if she was aware that adding this step to the routine would result in our being late for *Storytime*. But she gladly agreed to accept the consequences, since she is so very taken with the nature of all things toilet.

While waving a fond farewell to her poo, we discussed how much better she is feeling now that she is no longer taking 2 or more hours to poo. Again I explained to her that even though she misses having the larger amount of milk more often each day, the combination of less milk and her medicine seem to be helping her body to work more effectively, so that she can feel less pain and be less exhausted. As unsavoury as this topic of conversation is in some circles, I feel strongly that parents must be clear with their kids about how their bodies function or malfunction, so that kids can process the information and store it in order to help them manage capably in different situations.

Anica's resistance to the transition from one activity to the other gained strength as we approached the car and her seat inside. When I finally put her into her seat she arched her back and executed some impressive contortions in order to fight my attempts to secure her in her seatbelt. However, within a mere minute she had relaxed into a game centred around the new coat that I had dug out of the closet to replace the drenched one from earlier in the day; happily engaged in considering if the coat would go on her head, her toes, her knees, or over her eyes she was successfully distracted from our previous battle of wills. For the moment, I released an enormous internal sigh of relief as she cheerfully tried to decide which it would be, before moving on to explore the new pockets and snaps which she had not yet investigated.

As we drove up to the library I spied the massive strollers belonging to the daycares clogging up the bike rack again and was grateful that we hadn't raced up on our bike only to find nowhere to park it and the trailer. As soon as we sat down at the back of the group, Anica appeared sufficiently engrossed in the action songs for me to pull out my pen and notepad and try and catch up on my transcribing. As I tried to shift back into work mode, I noted that she was so cute stretching up on her tiptoes to try and see the librarian over the heads of all the big kids who had arrived at the library on time. Unfortunately, I paid for this lapse in my subterfuge when Anica noticed my pen and paper and asked for her own. Highly unsatisfied when I tried to suggest that she focus on *Storytime*, she looked at me accusingly, clearly branding me as a complete hypocrite. Thankfully it wasn't long before she was completely engrossed by acting out *Storytime Tea*, so that I could return to my reflections.

In no time at all, I was shifting my focus to the surprisingly short attention span of the toddler: one moment the ceiling fan was mesmerizing her and the next she was in the thick of a group stampeding for hand stamps. Thank goodness my kids have no TV, I thought, since I don't know what I would do with them if they had even higher expectations of constantly shifting modes of entertainment than they already do as a result of play dates and other weekly extra-curricular activities.

Leaving the library we were in a rush to pick up my prescription from the pharmacy on the way to collect Naia. As usual, we took the path of least resistance, our vehicle becoming like water in seeking the most direct path through the rocks (the latter symbolizing the proverbial construction zones, backed up traffic, and traffic calmed areas). Thankfully, the parking gods showed us favour by granting us 'rock star parking' right at the entranceway to the store. As soon as I loaded Anica into the cart, she made a plea for the candy displayed front and centre, and I reflected that it was a good thing she hadn't accompanied me here the evening before when I came to stock up Bobby's and my candy supply and completely forgetting to pick-up my prescription. At this point,

I found myself grateful for Naia's bottomless pit of a stomach which has trained me to always have snack on hand; to my relief Anica conceded that the apple pieces stowed in the bottom of my purse were a satisfactory enough consolation, this time.

Despite having overstayed our parking limit we managed to avoid getting a ticket and arrived at school on time for the third day in a row. Of course, all was not perfection, as we spent virtually the entire ten-minute trip to the school with Anica gnashing her teeth and wailing for the remaining apple that I couldn't reach while driving. I wouldn't be surprised if statistics showed that more mothers have accidents while a child inconsolably screamed for their snack from the back seat.

When we arrived at school I realized that I had gotten myself into yet another bind, acting out of a place of guilt rather than common sense. Due to my conflicting demands of teaching, studying, and childcare I haven't been scheduling as many play dates for my daughters as I would have done in the past. Therefore, I arranged 3 play dates over the course of 4 days, but even before starting the 2nd one I knew that I would be exhausted by the end of the week. At the same time, I began mulling over the further guilt I would experience just to coordinate each of these play dates. Since we don't have room to ferry any other kids in our car or our bike trailer, the other kids' moms or nannies would have to bring them to our house and pick them up, thereby contravening the whole point of a play date for most moms: having the chance not to have to worry about ferrying your kids here and there and enjoying an even longer stretch of luxurious peace and relaxation! The final onslaught of guilt hit me when I noted that the "biking goddess" (the only kindergarten mom who bikes in even the most inclement weather and always looks great doing it) was waiting at the entrance to the playground surrounded by her band of admiring biking dads. Sanity, I remind myself regularly, is more important than daily maintaining one's *image*.

After another bout of wrestling Anica into the car seat, we only just made it home before Naia's friend arrived for their play date. However, the race was not without casualties: in the struggle for the choice items to carry inside from the car, Naia's umbrella, purchased only two short months earlier, got a snapped spine. At least a measure of the potential drama was avoided in the heightened anticipation surrounding B's arrival. As the last seconds ticked down, I dove to wipe off the crusty table, only to hear the doorbell sound and my girls screech around the corner to the front door. While B's nanny was gushing effusively over our "beautiful house", I suppressed my desire to unload about its sieve-like state, and sought to recover my grasp on the many blessings we have in our home and in our affluence, compromising by innocuously muttering, "Yes, it's great for kids."

As soon as the door shut on B's nanny, the kids and I entered into what is known as: *the great lunch negotiations.* After my opening 4 sallies were shot down without a single pause for breath, I tried to recover while being pummeled by a series of requests for food items we didn't have. Finally, I scrounged for my keys to the garage in an effort to search out a tin of acceptable soup and when I came back empty-handed, I learned that my initial offer had been accepted and I could set to work in peace. Wryly, I reflected that at least I didn't have to worry about having kosher food today, like Naia's friend had spontaneously requested during yesterday's play date. However, before I bowed my head to the task of lunch prep, I negotiated my own contract terms, ensuring that the kids would tidy-up the clothes that already littered the entire surface of Naia's bedroom floor and in which they were planning to dress-up.

Once I announced that lunch was prepared, the entire pride of lions descended the stairs and proceeded to pounce on their food before it could escape. Undaunted by their predatory behaviour, I intervened in an effort at hygiene only to be rebuffed and told that they had already washed their hands. Even when I reminded them that I had just seen them doing one another's hair, B retorted that they had since washed up. Seeing the shock on Naia's face at this blatant lie gave me a measure of hope that my child was yet naive enough to be read like a book when seeking to dissemble. Rather than go head-to-head with them in this instance, I let it go and had a good chuckle at the worry still etched on Naia's features as she climbed onto her chair. Ravenously, those two scrawny vultures devoured 15 pieces of bread with avocado and cream cheese between them, along with as many vegetable bits as I could throw at them. All the while the little 'chubby bunny', nibbled at her veggie sticks and picked at her half slice of bread with cream cheese.

Once the older girls had raced away from the table, Anica happily occupied herself with swaddling her highly favoured, and ancient, Tickle-Me-Elmo before bundling him into her stroller and setting off for a walk around our house. Within seconds, the calm was shattered after she banged her head on the doorframe when taking the corner too fast. Screaming bloody murder, she brought the older girls running with alarm, only to greet them with a wooden chair that she whipped across the room. Holding back a desire to emit a belly laugh at her ridiculous display of temper (which eerily reminded me of my dad), I got down to her level and sought to console her over her sore head. Once she started to settle down, I endeavoured to impress upon her how dangerous it was to throw a chair regardless of the preceding events. Not surprisingly, it was quite clear that she thought I was batty for believing and explaining that it is unacceptable to express yourself in that way when you are hurt or angry; apparently, she thought it ludicrous that anyone would want to talk about or reflect on their feelings rather than take them out on the rest of the world.

Calm, if not bewildered, Anica returned to wheeling Elmo around, freeing me to get her bedroom ready for nap time in order to both accelerate the process and ease her into the next transition. Struggling under a load of stuff for the 2nd floor, I considered how this habit remains one of my sanity-saving strategies, maintaining some semblance of order in our home, and preventing it from becoming a kid-ruled environment. Quickly following on that thought, I noticed that the seedlings which Naia and I had planted a few weeks ago needed to be put outside during these daylight hours in order to harden their stems and leaves in preparation for planting outdoors thereby restoring our tub to an adult zone again. When putting out the plant trays, I was reminded that when I was bringing in the plants in last night my step-sister had called, but since I had just started the girls' nighttime routine, I was sufficiently distracted to forget to call her back as I had promised. I reflected that at least it was only 1 more item to add to a 'to do' list advancing well into the double digits.

Returning to the first floor to give Anica her cup of milk I was treated to a fashion show exhibiting Naia's clothing collection. This gave me the chance to tell Naia and B that they had one more outfit they could choose before they needed to tidy up the clothes. "At that point," I explained, "I will have gotten Anica in bed and it will be time for our new activity". My use of these *word cues* were part of my effort to remind Naia of our preplanned 'big girl' project. As Anica savoured the last few sips of her 'moo' juice, I lingered over my 'under-the-radar treat', the hot chocolate that I had picked up from Blenz the night before. Even though it had been Bobby's idea to get them, enjoying my own was a surprising pick-me-up in a day that primarily had focused on taking care of everyone else. I think that I can understand why so many moms are loathe to sacrifice their coffee at Starbucks (or whichever pricey joint they frequent), since there are very few things that allow a mom to spoil herself in the course of an otherwise long and demanding day.

When Anica and I arrived in the upstairs bathroom, I remembered that it was laundry time again. Doing laundry in our house has transformed into a team effort that serves to provide Anica with a challenge with which she can feel successful and at the same time helps me to prevent things from literally piling up. The work is divided as follows: I sort the laundry, Anica finds the stains, together we put the stain remover on them, then she puts the clothes into the machine. After a short five minutes, everything is soaking in the machine and she is more cooperative to engage in whatever activity we need to do next. Sometimes, however, I am somewhat frustrated by this process, not because she drags it out or makes it inefficient, something I used to stress about, but rather that the green laundry products we now use, do a rotten job of actually getting most stains out. Hopefully soon, a group of friends and I will buy the ingredients in bulk and make our own products so as to save money and also find more effective recipes.

Now that the bedtime routine was well underway, I realized that I still had to throw the poopy clothing soaking in the tub into the machine and had to clear away last night's tubby toys drying on the edge of the bath. However, I had to be quick if I didn't want to lose Anica to another distracting activity before bedtime. Today I was lucky enough to get her toothbrush in her hand and engage her in brushing along to *The Toothbrush Family* song and Raffi's "When I wake up in the morning..."

Of course, all was not without conflict. When it came time to choose her book and we were deep into negotiations she suddenly shifted gears and asked for a bottle. Despite the fact that she had already drunk her milk from a cup, she was distraught at not having a second helping in a baby bottle. She still derives a lot of comfort from sucking on a bottle, but since she has a tendency to whip them when she is finished we haven't bought glass bottles nor returned our old bottles for 'safe' plastic ones. Although

31

I am in no rush to take away a form of comfort for Anica, I loathe getting sucked into a buying frenzy for the new wave of *healthy* products for children. In fact, in our attempts to move away from plastic kids' dishes we have experimented with existing ceramic, stainless steel, and wood dishes rather than buying new replacement 'safe' plastic ones. It is so overwhelming, and shockingly expensive to try and be a discerning parent consumer, but we are trying to hold to our frugal and conservative habits in the midst of this insanity.

Thankfully she abandoned her fixation on the bottle and ran to the bathroom yelling, "POTTY"! Unfortunately, because of the abrupt change of topic, I was left behind in her dust and arrived only in time to find a pool of pee on the floor. While I was reassuring her that it was a great try and was trying to help her climb onto the potty seat to see if she had anymore pee left, she started pushing at me, saying "Mama, pee? Please?" I obliged her and laughed to myself as she heartily cheered at my success, exuberantly flushing the toilet before I was able to stand. The latter action, her goal all along, having been now achieved, she swung into hand washing with vigour. Since she knows that she is not allowed to flush the toilet unless there is a more substantial amount of waste in it, she has become a 'pee solicitor' in order to get her thrill while also adhering to the household rule to save water.

Returning to her room to read a book, we entered into final book selection negotiations before she returned the rejects to our room so that she couldn't pull a fast one on me, sneaking in multiple stories before bedtime. At this point, she switched into her sister's tried and true attempt at delay tactics before bed. Trying to stall by engaging me in *a conversation* about Bobby, she asked, "Dada?" To which I responded, "He's working." But when she said, "Sushi?" she threw me for a loop. Confused, I inquired, "What?" And then stated, "No, he works at the hospital where he helps people to feel better." Insistent, she pushed for, "Sushi?" At which I point I tried, "No sweetie, Dada doesn't make sushi." Apparently having cleared up that misunderstanding, she emitted a simple, "Oh." That topic exhausted, I managed to cuddle her for her bedtime song, and then as I lifted her into her crib she began to laugh hysterically and say "Side, side". I suddenly realized that she found it funny to be put into the opposite side of her bed now that we have had to move it out from under the alternately dripping and flaking ceiling. Settling, she said, "Noonie, noon", and cuddled all of her *lovies*, including her *mama shirt* (the acceptable replacement for my underwear which she initially wanted whenever I was out of her reach) and her baby sheep. To clarify a regular matter of confusion, her precious sheep's name is not 'Baabaa', as most people assume, but rather 'Bubba', Naia's second choice for a boy's name when I was pregnant with Anica (her first choice being another unusual name: 'Ingo', after her uncle's friend).

Quickly I returned downstairs to the two older girls and found them trying to hook-up a toy which both my husband and I despair of for a variety of reasons: it devours battery power, requires specially-designed and separately purchased paper, as well as making a nasty mess of everyone's hands, clothes, and the surface on which it rests. After asking them what they should have done before attempting to set up this toy (to which the girls responded "Ask and wait for adult help"), I shifted the emphasis to their taking responsibility for the clean-up and preparation for the activity which we had previously agreed upon. Naia's determination became immediately apparent: fixated on whether or not I would hold up my end of the bargain and get the replacement paper for this trendy toy (please note the disdain in my voice when I say "trendy"), she would not transition to the next activity. When I explained that the paper is a costly item and that very few stores carry it, she persisted until I gave her a clear answer about when I would *attempt* to purchase the paper (I did not allow myself to be boxed into promising that I *would* buy the paper on that occasion thereby allowing myself some wiggle room in case it was too expensive or she had lost interest in the activity once we reached that deadline).

Breathing a sigh of relief as I saw them tidy up the other toy and materials, I fetched the molding clay and floor mat. Soon we were all engrossed in a project that Naia and I had started the previous week that entailed making small clay flowers for her grandmothers. Despite it being past mother's day, I persisted in completing this project with her since I knew the grandmas would appreciate them and she would get lots of satisfaction out of, 1) seeing her work finished, and 2) hearing the recipients' excitement upon their receiving their gifts.

Once we wrapped up our clay project and I began preparing their snack, Naia proceeded to give me a fright by jumping out at me dressed as a pirate and yelling

"ARRGGHH"! In my shock, I was very terse with her for doing it and especially for being so loud during her sister's naptime. I know that I am tired when I dwell too much on the noise level of my kids and don't think about what is the real source of my anger. In this case, I am sure that I was very startled and that I overreacted as a result. However, I got my just desserts when Naia became very hurt and embarrassed by my display of anger in front of her friend. Her friend, for her part, was unconcerned by the tension between us and remarked upon leaving that she "felt she had spent the whole day at our house"! When I inquired if that was "a good or a bad thing", she hastily said that it was "great because she had never had any time to be bored or wonder what time it was". Thankfully, the two girls parted with big hugs and huge grins, leaving me certain that we would see B again in the not too distant future.

Yet, the instant the door closed behind her friend, Naia began crying and pleading with me *not* to leave "since [she] would miss me when [I] went to work". As our nanny arrived, she then went on to insist that she *really didn't* need a rest, but could go to bed early instead. Her tiredness revealed the *Negotiator* snuggled up to me sobbing that she was "not at all tired", but "just need[ed] to have a cuddle with [me] to feel better". Late in the day as it was at that point, I acquiesced to her requests while securing a commitment from both her, and from our nanny, Dopé, that she would go to bed early. After our cuddle Naia scooted happily over to the table for her snack while I escaped upstairs to make corrections to my reflections.

Unfortunately, I still needed to attend to household matters first. After booting up my computer, I noted that the roofing company wanted to come to redo the work that they had screwed up, right in the middle of Anica's naptime the next day. Furthermore, while they were conceding that the work needed repair, and were giving me a day's notice about when they might be coming (it was good to see this after having requested it literally a dozen times previously), I had no guarantee that they would actually do the job properly this time since they were planning to send the same repairman without a supervisor AGAIN. Sighing deeply, I requested a morning time and a visit from a supervisor to make an account of the repairs to date. One can only hope, right? Next I reviewed the estimate from the restoration company and was pleased to see that they had revised it exactly as we had requested, causing me to forward it on to Bobby so that we could discuss it that night and approve it before morning. As I sent a quick email to my best friend inquiring whether our visits home to Ontario this summer were likely to overlap so that I could confirm our flight dates, I realized that I was running behind and needed to get changed and race off to the university, having no time to make any headway on my work.

When I approached my bedroom I found Naia lurking in the hallway outside, hoping to catch me before I left. I told her to join me while I changed after which she carefully approved each item of my attire and ensured that I was suitably accessorized before gathering my bags. Seeing me note our interactions as I went downstairs, she scolded me for wasting paper (which her dad and I regularly find ourselves saying to her sister and her), after which I informed her that it is not wasting paper when you have a clear purpose for every piece you are using. The footnote to this comment being that I did since it was for my schoolwork about which I would be meeting my advisor within the hour!

On that point she conceded defeat, and instead turned to inquiring about my intentions for feeding myself between my meeting and my class. When I told her that she could get me an apple, she informed me that an apple was "not enough" and that I needed "a proper meal". Dopé and I laughed until I struggled to the door, closing it behind me, while Naia waved goodbye to me through the window. As I lugged my many bags to the car, I reflected that I was very glad for her diminutive stature, so that at least I still had one advantage over her!

As I drove out to the University to meet with my academic advisor, I reflected on how unprepared I felt to meet with her. Despite my best intentions to immerse myself in books from my reading list and arrive at our appointment having a greater sense of perspective about what direction my practicum was taking me in, I hadn't even managed to email her a copy of my meager point form notes from my various parent education sessions thus far. While I am certain that my vocation in life is a joint one of parent, wife, and adult educator, I realize that I will likely always struggle with the toll that each takes on me and on the additional roles that I live out on a daily basis. Furthermore, I know that if I don't engage in a regular practice of questioning my habits and musing on the interplay of each of my roles, I am likely to find myself struggling with significant self-doubt and self-recrimination. Thankfully, I know that sessions like this one planned with Shauna help me enormously to air my thoughts and feel newly inspired to resume the juggling act once again. Sadly, on this occasion Shauna and I had gotten our wires crossed and I was unable to meet with her before having to head off to teach my evening class at the Adler Centre. Despite my initial disappointment, I used the time while I was waiting to make corrections to my reflections in the peaceful child-free zone of the university. Furthermore, on my way to teach I even had time to pick-up a sticky treat for my students and eat a yummy fish taco while reading the newspaper--what a luxury!

　　While setting up my classroom with my co-facilitator, we were informed that we had to be quieter before, during, and after our classes in order not to disturb the counseling sessions under way in the adjacent offices. Almost halfway through our eight-week program, we were surprised at receiving these ultimatums from the office manager on behalf of the counselors. My colleague and I laughed at how odd humans are; we mused about how strange it was that the counselors felt that they could not have spoken to us directly about their concerns earlier on in the program, choosing instead to make the situation more complex in order to achieve their desired end. While we both always make it a priority for our classes to be fun and interactive we also make an effort to be respectful of others with whom we share the facilities. On this occasion we reinforced our usual practice by making a special note of the need to be quiet upon arrival, during breaks, and at wrap-up time, so as to impress on our students the heightened sensitivity of our neighbours.

　　During our class time discussion, I felt affirmed when we reviewed the question of why children act in negative ways, though positive options might be available to them. Our discussion clarified for me that Naia had been acting out of her discouragement with the physical and emotional distance between us as of late when she had lashed out at me first and then clung to me following my emotional withdrawal. I was also encouraged that, before I left home, we had made a date for the next day, during which we planned to spend some quiet time together one-on-one. As soon as I had made that commitment to her I saw Naia visibly brighten and her steps lighten and I had known that she would not make another scene now that she was feeling more hopeful and relaxed in anticipation.

Upon returning home at 9:30 pm, I found Bobby just finishing his dinner and, I thought, 'vegging out' in front of the computer. Though he is rarely tempted by the idea of having a television, except possibly when FIFA World Cup Soccer is on, I, on the other hand, miss the more entertaining format of television, over and against email and the mostly printed word with which we both occupy our time on our computers. While I occasionally watch my favourite satires, like "The Rick Mercer Report", or insightful dramas, such as "Six Feet Under", Bobby is more likely to spend an evening engrossed in reviewing and compiling emails about his second full-time job, the gelato company he jointly owns with two others and which is located in the San Francisco Bay Area. Indeed arriving home that night, I learned that he had actually been spending his night, 1) engaging in a conference call with his fellow partners and general manager, 2) researching and scheduling appointments with International Tax Accountants, and 3) endeavouring to plan a restructuring of the company which could finally allow us to claim the business losses which we have been unable to for the last five years.

Greeted with this news, I felt my energy draining out of my body. At times it has felt as though the two of us lead completely separate existences, with our passions and priorities overlapping only periodically. Before sharing with him the revelations which I had discovered through recording my thoughts, interactions, and events of my day, I found myself aware that yet again he has shouldered his own enormous burdens and has expended his energies in very different, yet no less challenging ways than I.

Usually up and out of the house before the girls and I even wake in the morning, he bikes downtown to greet his patients, review their charts, prep the OR, and brief his residents, anesthesia underway before the girls and I have even finished dressing and eating. His long days and, at times, the high cost of the decisions he regularly must make take a toll on him, though he is well-rewarded for his attention to detail and is very well-regarded for his work-ethic and caring manner.

In contrast, I struggle to find worldly significance in what I do. One moment I rant and rave at the unjust dismissal of the sheer amount of physical, emotional, and creative energy that I expend daily in an effort to understand, engage with, and rally behind my kids and my spouse and the next moment I am convinced that I am not doing enough. I often find myself discouraged by the lack of value that the discourses on motherhood grant to my work and their expectation that I should juggle even more. This parallels the conflicting discourses on fathering and work that demand Bobby give more and more all the time to both of these parts of his life with little consideration for himself (see Wall & Arnold 2007; Kugelberg 2006; Milner 2010; Featherstone 2003).

As time passes Bobby and I are getting better at crossing over the artificial boundaries that delineate our roles both within and without the family; together we are exploring new ways in which we can re-imagine ourselves as mother and father to Naia and Anica while still caring for one another within the context of our marriage and our external working roles. Thankfully tonight, we managed to bridge the divide and find the common ground between our two vocations, committing to listen to and support one another as learners, carers, and teachers despite the distinct responsibilities we carry that often position us at odds from one another.

Epilogue: Sunday, October 26*th*, 2008 12:22 am

Naia and Anica,

It is, approximately, the one-year anniversary of my written promise to you, although I didn't realize it until tonight. When I came across my letter to you earlier this evening, I was struck by how my commitment to you has largely defined both my public and private self over the course of the last year, a fact for which I am truly grateful. I have invested our relationship with new depth and resources by investing myself in my mothering role through daily attendance to you and through examining my mothering past and future in the context of my graduate studies. In doing so I am becoming a mother learner who recognizes that neither I, nor the systems and structures in which I mother, will ever be perfect (Kinser 2008a, p. 1, 6). Despite this I will persevere.

I have also begun to come to terms with the challenge each new day brings: the sleep I am craving, the deadlines I must meet, the illnesses I am fighting, and the support I am lacking. While I was reluctant to reveal my parenting insecurities and shrank away from many opportunities to share my experiences and impressions for fear of shame and criticism, increasingly I have spoken and written about my story and my perceptions of its significance. This risk has afforded me greater affirmation as a mother, an educator, and a learner, and in turn, I have discovered a wealth of opportunities for connection, intimacy, and healing with you and others.

By grace, I am able to empathize with, encourage, and inspire mothers and fathers to envision new possibilities for learning, living, and being using the tools of humour, insight, and mutual understanding to guide me. My writing and learning is living that is not just rational and analytical but sensual, physical, emotional, psychological, and spiritual--"it is a writing that heightens the senses, tastes life twice, in the present moment and in the retrospection" (Dunlop 1998, p. 122).

Motherhood: Myths

As evidenced by the previous narrative, the images of motherhood and mothering bombard us in our society, particularly via the media. These social constructions make it difficult to discern what motherhood consists of and what makes it worthwhile. Since these conceptions of mothering so often focus on what lies on the surface, rather than either on the particular children who inspire their parents or on how momentary challenges may grant us crucial insight into ourselves and into our capacity to persevere, we mother learners are often left focusing on superficial concerns.

Being "preoccupied with material necessity" I easily succumb to meeting the immediate demands of mothering, such as feeding, clothing, and entertaining my children, rather than diligently nurturing my relationships with them (Grumet 1988, p. 106). Judging the value of my relationships according to the world's terms of value and "recompense", I have tended to focus on what I *am not doing*, what I *am not earning* rather than the substantive value of what I *am providing*, *gaining*, and *have to contribute* as a mother (Grumet 1988, p. 57; 15; Daly 2004, p. 8, 11; Tuley 2008, p. 159; Ehrenreich & English 2005, p. 232, 297; Horowitz & Long 2005, p. 99; Reid-Boyd 2005, p. 199). In the moment of mothering I desire a sense of satisfaction that is fleeting rather than trusting that the true value of mothering lies in the development and growth of the bonds between my children and myself.

Consumer Choice: All Blush and Bluster

I do not aspire to yummy mummyhood
until I see a store window, a mirror, or a webpage
which offers up a slew of choice lifestyle options
to those who wield a never-ending supply of cash.

Very little inspiration is to be found
in slings and snugglies and sweet potato mash,
in body-hugging workout wear or rockabilly togs for toddlers.
Instead my creative juices flow
from the joy, angst, and sorrow bound up in kith and kin.

Context: Transitioning from Daughter to Wife and Mother

As I look back on the beginnings of my conscious mother learning process, I see myself on the verge of motherhood, a young woman, the daughter of a broken marriage, the wife of a conscientious and hard-working man, wrestling with how I might find my way despite my vision being clouded by expectation and fear, as well as by hope and sorrow. As I prepared myself for the birth of my first child, I was earnestly attempting to shift my focus to my new life role but I did so with trepidation because of the radical changes that I presumed lay ahead of me. I was also aware that some of my uncertainty lay in my inability to discern what I must do to adapt myself to this path.

To begin with, I worried that I was not worthy of the opportunity to care for the child in my womb. From the moment I began to miscarry during my first pregnancy, I doubted my suitability for the vocation of mothering and these doubts haunted me for some time to come. In my haste to become pregnant a second time, I did not allow myself enough time to grieve for my first child, or for the hope that I had lost in the process. My distress was compounded by morning sickness from week 5 of my second pregnancy and, while trying to find a balance between the constant nausea and drowsiness, which was a side effect of treatment, I continued to feel that I was a failure in the eyes of my doctor, who implied that every pound that I gained would result in a catastrophe.

As the pregnancy progressed my doctor retracted her prediction of excessive weight gain, instead declaring that I must eat more often and in greater quantities, especially more protein. Confused, I requested a referral to a nutritionist, who helped me to regain some perspective on my eating habits by restoring a more creative rather than clinical approach to food preparation and consumption.

Unfortunately, my doctor became alarmed once again. This time it was the low levels of amniotic fluid that alarmed her. Together with the disproportionate rate of growth between my fetus' head, trunk, and limbs, this caused her to elect to put me on bed rest for the last two months of my pregnancy and to refer me to a specialist for ongoing care and the delivery of my baby. She also scheduled regular ultrasounds to monitor the baby's growth in utero.

41

These complications meant that I had to give up my professional role and my community precipitously and caused me to question my identity from a number of different perspectives, among them: where would I find value now that I was no longer a paid teacher and counselor; to whom would I turn for support and companionship; and, would I be fulfilled enough solely as a mother and wife? As the wife of a medical resident I had already spent the last 5 years wrestling with the societal affirmation given to those who conscientiously work long hours and earn larger salaries for their public roles. In contrast, I wondered where my satisfaction and affirmation would come from changing diapers hourly, ensuring the laundry was washed and folded, the meals prepared, and the house cleaned.

Suddenly with a great deal of free time, I began to realize how isolated I had become from my family and long term friendships; not only could I not overcome the distance that separated me from most of them simply by way of telephone or email, but I perceived that I had yet to heal from recent wounds that I had endured. My miscarriage had occurred only four months after the death of my beloved maternal grandmother and 8 months after learning that my mother was facing her second bout with cancer: none of which I had begun to process, let alone become reconciled to in the interim. In addition, my husband was consumed with preparing for his professional exams in 8 months time.

I suspected that I was inviting my child to inhabit a fragile time, and a space that was just as bereft. Girding myself, I resolved not to yield to my fears, believing that as independent, accomplished, and strong as I had been to date I must continue to persevere.

Without Peers and Without an Empowered Mothering Model

As a new mother I believed that somehow I innately ought to know how to be a mother: when to address my child's many needs and desires and when to choose my own well being over her expectations (Ehrenreich & English 2005, p. 243). But it did not come naturally to me to shift from doing what I wanted, or only what Bobby and I wanted, to that of only what my child wanted, especially when that was in direct conflict with my, and/or our, desires (Horowitz & Long 2005, p. 100, 102; Bobel 2008, p. 120; Aragon 2008, p. 171; O'Brien Hallstein 2008, p. 107).

From observing, rather than questioning, two of my four friends who already had children of their own, I perceived that the standard for mothers was to be patient, highly competent, creative, and satisfied. The only other mothers I knew that did not exude this same self-assurance were two women already facing failing marriages, causing me to feel as though my concerns were not significant enough to warrant additional attention and support.

As a result of my assumptions about my mother-friends falling into one of only two categories of mothers, I was convinced that no one else had needed to go through the transition from being, or at least feeling, an inadequate and ignorant mother to becoming a competent and knowledgeable one as I believed I needed to do. Instead I thought that these mothers must have always *innately known* how to be "good" mothers but were forced from their known path through no fault of their own (Hays 1998, p. 14; Ehrenreich & English 2005, p. 357-358; Marotta 2008). This resulted in my feeling as though I might forever remain the inadequate and ignorant mother, the "bad" mother that I felt myself to be and that society would label me as for my selfish thoughts and inclinations (Ladd-Taylor & Umansky 1998, p. 1-21; O'Brien Hallstein 2008, p. 107, 111).

What I didn't learn until years later was that both of the mother friends whom I had esteemed at this point in my mother learning process had struggled with their own sense of failure in their mothering role, particularly with respect to the quantity and the quality of time and energy that they invested in their relationships with their children. As a relatively new mother, I still did not realize how accomplished many mothers can be at presenting a facade of proficiency and ease with their daily life.

The belief *that women are born to motherhood naturally*, rather than being confined by a socio-cultural construct and a set of self-imposed duties, permeated my decision not to ask for further familial support until after I had sought out counseling (Rich 1986, p. 276). Embarrassed by the looks of, what I perceived to be, disbelief and dismay on Bobby's face at seeing me flail about in those early weeks of mothering Naia, I kept my fears and my plans to get help to myself. Instead of considering that he or other family and friends might have wisdom, encouragement, and/or other forms of assistance that they could share with me, I thought that others could only really *perform* a supporting role by *doing* things for Naia and for me. However, because of limitations imposed by work demands, distance, and/or their own family responsibilities, I concluded that I ought not to ask for help from those I already knew (Butler 2004).

While at first I dismissed any idea that I might be dealing with postpartum depression, once I was diagnosed with having anxiety disorder triggered by my postpartum experiences I began to realize that I was internalizing many of the external discourses that I had encountered both prior to becoming a mother and during my early months of motherhood and that these discourses were negatively influencing my mothering experience. I recognized that I needed to relinquish the desire to control all of my time, energy, and priorities by acquiring a learner's attitude to mothering and womanhood: a mindset that would take considerable conscious effort to adopt (Chandler 1998; Smith 1987). Resolving to abandon my resentments and celebrate the joys of being a mother, I struck out to discern how I might find mothering possibilities that would enable me to bridge this tension in the moment and the paradoxes of mothering over the long term.

I Am Raw: A Mother at War with Her Memory of Self

An agent of
indiscreet
practices
alone
within society
inhabiting a body
of intimacy
and self-ness less

made amorphous
by risk
and dis-conversations
of undentity

Are we all vulnerable
to shame
or just mothers?

Mother Learning: A Counter-Discourse

My research, which has an autobiographical impetus, has its roots in Michel Foucault's concept of *critique*. Critique, Foucault (1984a) insists, requires a deliberate effort to isolate the links between knowledge and power and to substantiate both their "contents" and their "effects" (p. 49-50). I posit that not only do parents need to question the intransigence and self-serving nature of externally-imposed mothering and fathering models, but increasingly they must resist the dominance of these *parenting discourses* by not remaining "subordinate" to these ideals and patterns by seeking alternate ways of knowing (Foucault 1984a, p. 32). Such *counter-discourses* are developed via skeptical "thinking, speaking, and acting" (p. 24-25). These necessarily non-totalizing and non-universal responses function outside of current norms as alternative possibilities regarding: *who mothers/fathers are, what families are,* and *how to mother/father.*

The relationship between these elements of knowledge is reflected in Foucault's (1984a) description of *critical inquiry.* From a search for the roots of knowledge to a "historical ontology of ourselves", Foucault explores how we are shaped by external discourses and how we "constitute ourselves" (p. 45-46). In so doing, he bridges the gap between what is past and what is "possible" in the context of our *self-formation* (Rabinow 1984, p. 11). Through our thoughts, words and actions, Foucault argues that we assert our knowing and our "being" within and without the confines of temporal and social contexts (Foucault 1984a, p. 63). At the same time, we "test the limits" of when, where, and how certain roles, such as mother, father, eldest, middle and youngest children, are all enacted (Foucault 1984b p. 46-47).

Judith Butler (2004) also incites individuals to create counter-discourses through *critical awareness* in her chapter, "Beside Oneself: On the Limits of Sexual Autonomy" (pp. 17-39). By extending the boundaries of what is identifiable as beyond what traditional discourses claim, she exhorts individuals to challenge the authority of *experts* to "label and categorize" individuals, families, and communities (p. 30-32; see also Moussa & Scapp 1996, p. 108). Foucault (1984a) articulated that resistance and critique, in particular, are creative; critique is an action that expands the realm of the possible, by questioning and substituting alternatives (p. 16). He calls individuals to resist governance and its efforts to "retool" us for its proprietary purposes (Fairclough 1992, p. 9).

In this essay I will use critique to question both the validity of the traditional sources of mother knowledge and the resultant discourses that validate particular parent identities and practices. I will establish both *the home* and *the community* as dynamic sites of mother learning that are mobile and interactive and serve as vital sites of social critique through the development of *counter-discourses*. I will counter the predominance of western, patriarchal parent education by documenting *mother learning* as an alternative possibility for *knowing*, *living* and *being* (Hart 1992, p. 24; Segura 1994, p. 212; Hill Collins 1994, p. 59).

Whether through personal and/or familial migration, *many* Canadian mothers and fathers of my generation have experienced dislocation from both immediate and extended family networks. This has made the traditional apprenticeship models of mother learning a physical impossibility and resulted in a learning vacuum for those of us preparing to have, and having, children (Man 2001 p. 428). Within this vacuum, numerous so-called 'experts' from a variety of disciplines have emerged and have claimed to possess ultimate knowledge of *best* parenting practices (Dobson 1983; Sears & Sears 2001; Murkoff, et al. 2003; Leach 1997; Ehrenreich & English 2005; Nathanson & Tuley 2008).

By branding their knowledge as 'superior', the marketing machines of these experts have targeted a select group of consumers for their product (Foley 1999, p. 69). Rather than affirming and fostering discussions about a diversity of parent/child relationships, these experts have identified a narrow category of familial relationships as valid models of *mothering*, *fathering*, and *families*.

Excluded by discourses which reify existing power structures, parents who are, for example, single, immigrant, disabled, homosexual, and/or working, are often depicted as lacking the resources to provide adequately for their children because of their perceived financial, socio-cultural, physical, or interpersonal inadequacies (Green 2004, p. 31; Segura 1994, p. 212; Hill Collins 1994, p. 59). I would argue that these discourses alienate not only what these experts would have us believe is the periphery of society, but also those of us who wish to avoid participating in either a consumerist or a crisis aversion model of parenting. By labeling certain of us as *others*, as social misfits, because we do not behave and feel as they have instructed us to, these experts exclude many of us from the parenting discourse (Marotta 2008, p. 210).

> The woman who felt sick, depressed, or simply tired would no longer
> seek help from a friend or female healer, but from a male physician. The
> general theory that guided the doctors' practice as well as their public
> pronouncements was that women were, by nature, weak, dependent,
> and diseased ... woman's essential nature was not to be a strong,
> competent help-giver, but to be a *patient*." (italics in original) (Ehrenreich
> & English 2005, p. 113)

As a new mother a number of years ago, I felt disempowered by health-mandated parenting discourses that portrayed any measure of difference in either children or their parents as pathological (Dobson 1983; Sears & Sears 2001; Murkoff, et al. 2003; Leach 1997). While striving to incorporate each and every trend and model of parenting strategies provided for my consumption, I found myself both confused and disheartened by my inability to master anything (Horowitz & Long 2005, p. 98). Initially I thought that I could not question the overwhelming sense I had that I was failing at mothering since I perceived myself as having every advantage: a supportive family, a stable home, a financially secure present and future, and parenting resources abounding. Gradually I discerned that the anxiety I experienced was not solely the result of my depressive disorder, but also a pattern of disempowerment perpetuated by mother-myth discourses and by encounters with caregivers who did not respond to me with sufficient caring or compassion (Pacific Postpartum Support Society 2002, p. 42-44, 53, 54; Ehrenreich & English 2005, p. 354).

The primary failing of many parenting models is that *by labeling particular parenting behaviours as one of two extremes*, either responsible or irresponsible, *their rhetoric seeks to impose value limitations on both mothering and fathering practices and in turn, on the parents themselves*. These models perpetuate in parents a fear of being labeled as a *bad* parent, as having failed their child (Marotta 2008, p. 210; Horowitz & Long 2005, p. 98; Ladd-Taylor & Umansky 1998, p. 1-21). By "constructing" *parents* in particular roles or identities, mothers and fathers can be manipulated as passive elements or instruments in the socially controlled processes prescribed by expert parenting discourses (Fairclough 1992, p. 208).

Alternatively, parents may be constructed as a "discerning customer or consumer" rather than remaining the more multidimensional person that they are on a daily basis (pp. 208-209). This is the box that I feel that I am being contained within when I read many of the mother resources in the grocery store lineups or on the internet (see wee.welcome.ca, canadianfamily.ca, or westcoastmoms.ca/wcm.ca as examples of this consumptive construction of parents).

In the process of *subjectifying* parents, these discourses regard them as *objects* whose customs and behaviour they scrutinize, and whose minds and wills they seek to "govern", while alienating them from particular physical and/or social contexts (Rabinow 1984, p. 8-11). In an attempt to create knowledge hegemonies, these discrete systems of power compete with one another, and at the same time, subjugate alternative knowledge claims (Foucault 1984a, p. 56). Since few, if any of us, are *always* excluded by normalizing discourses, we all share (although not equally) the burden of complicity with the resulting exclusion.

As a first-time mother I had never permitted myself to consider that it might be acceptable to find mothering difficult until on one of my initial visits my psychiatrist asked how I perceived the cost of caring for Naia. Hesitant at first, I was soon able to express that I found it extremely demanding to expend so much of my energy attending to both Naia's *needs* and her *desires*, particularly as I was unable to recognize the difference between them.

Following that conversation, many of our counseling sessions focused on how defeated I felt trying to meet the standards that I perceived were imposed upon mothers by society's unreasonable expectations. For example, as a new mother I was unable to discern the "balance and boundaries" which Dr. William Sears and Martha Sears (2001) describe in *The Eleven Commandments for Balanced Attachment Parenting* (p. 118).[2]

---

[2] These include as follows:
I. Thou shalt take care of thyself; II. Thou shalt honour they husband with his share of the attachment parenting; III. Thou shalt avoid the prophets of bad baby advice; IV. Thou shalt surround thyself with helpful and supportive friends; V. Thou shalt have help at home; VI. Thou shalt get to know thy baby; VII. Thou shalt give children what they need, not what they want; VIII. Thou shalt sleep when baby sleeps; VIIII. Thou shalt groom and adorn thyself; X. Thou shalt heal thy past; XI. Thou shalt realize thou art not perfect (Sears & Sears 2001, p. 118).

When reading through their list of directives I immediately felt that I was being expected to perform an impossible role; Sears and Sears do not acknowledge that these guidelines take far more subtle discernment, physical stamina, mental perseverance, and monetary resources than many parents, even two in the same family, can claim (p. 6, 106-118). I was confused by the inconsistency between these commandments that encouraged parents to focus on themselves and later parts of the same chapter that prioritized the needs of the baby. For example, the *7 B's of Attachment Parenting*, "birth bonding, breastfeeding, babywearing, bedding close to baby, belief in baby's cry, and beware of baby trainers", minimize the needs of the parents in contrast to those of the baby by emphasizing that the mother, and father, must submit themselves to caring for their child physically, emotionally, psychologically, and mentally, day and night (Sears 2001, p. 2-10).

Isolated by my self-doubt and the physical distance from my family and closest friends, I felt more criticized by these experts than supported and encouraged by them when I read that I ought to feel "blessed" by Naia's "high-need" temperament (Sears & Sears 2003, p. 413). Dr. and Mrs. Sears claimed that she would be more perceptive and assertive about what she wanted from life, and thereby more successful, because of her awareness of her surroundings and other people that already had been evident in her in infancy. Instead of feeling hopeful about this future, this prediction caused me to feel dismissed and ungrateful in the short term since it assumed too much insight and imposed a judgment on me for not always feeling or expressing the *right* emotions in response to her sensitivity. This conclusion also assumed that Naia would make the *right* decisions due to this sensitivity, a conclusion that I would propose is premature.

I now know that there is an alternate response to these expert discourses. By *questioning* the power hierarchies that create and are reinforced by these essentialist and totalizing discourses, mothers and fathers can destabilize the very idea of such unattainable ideals in order to unearth the "familiar, unchallenged, unconsidered modes of thought" that serve to undermine *original and reflective mothering and fathering practices* (Foucault, 1984a, p. 60; Foucault as cited by Olssen 1999, p. 134). This *resistance* is a crucial step in critically analyzing the parent learning process.

Eventually I began to be able to risk expressing "outlaw emotions" to Naia in the moment of our interactions (Jagger 1989, p. 166). By taking ownership of what Rich (2005) calls my "subversive emotions", I began to recognize where I needed to set some boundaries on my energy (p. 52). Once I was able to see *naming* my negative emotions was a necessary step that would benefit my children, and not just me, I could clarify for either of them the value of when and how *to give to*, and *not to just demand of, others* perpetually. The more affirmed I felt by my psychiatrist, my family, and my close friends the more I shared my challenges and insights with others until I was able to begin using my energies for *developing responsive, creative mothering practices* and not just coping strategies.

The opportunities granted me by my psychiatrist to consider and reconsider my thoughts and feelings affirmed me both as a mother and as a learner and enabled me to move beyond my personal doubts about external discourses and *to begin to articulate why I sought alternate approaches to mothering*. In doing this I claimed the ethical responsibility and the logistical means to question the processes that validate expert knowledge by developing what Foucault calls "a critical attitude" (Foucault 1984a p. 24).

I submit that parents must build on the narrow aspect of Mechthild Hart's (1992) premise that mothering is "work" necessarily defined by the "specially learned skills and demands" developed through attendance to their child's "needs" (p. 183-184). Despite Hart's attempts to resist reducing mothering to a consumptive model she does not prevent mothering from also being reduced to a mechanistic standard when she portrays children as items "produced" for the gratification of those in positions of authority (p. 176, 179). In this polarizing portrayal when she describes adults as possessing "mature" identities she risks limiting the child's agency within their family and she also fails to emphasize the dynamic, interpersonal nature of the parent-child relationship by implying that adults are not influenced by their children (p. 176).

Ultimately, I would argue that it is essential to recognize the inherently dynamic and humbling nature of parent-child interaction and of the parent learning and knowing processes. In contrast to Hart (1992), I would propose that both mothers and fathers must prioritize their *own* "needs" as well as considering the *child's* physical, mental, emotional, and spiritual welfare (p. 183-184). While in some cases children alone may determine the knowledge their parents seek, this pattern is not healthy for either the children or either parent over a lengthy period of time (Sheedy Kurcinka 1998, p. 2).

Following Naia's birth I sought to satisfy Naia's needs and desires almost exclusively. This pursuit was damaging to my physical, mental, emotional, psychological, and spiritual well being, as well as the health of my marriage. In that same time period Bobby had dedicated himself to fulfilling the virtually endless expectations of his final year of anesthesia residency, and I did not dare question his preoccupation with his work or mine with Naia until he and I began reflecting on how wildly divergent our daily lives and roles were as Naia approached 18 months of age. Only when a move to St. Louis for Bobby's fellowship training promised to uproot Naia and me from our tenuous ties to family and community support did I question whether Bobby's work might be requiring too much of us all.

I am so grateful that when I did question the conflict between his work expectations and my needs, Bobby gave up his job and his fellowship training post, risking the reputation for which he had worked the entire five years of his residency. He did this in order to do a year of fellowship training in Ontario, closer to our parents and to some of our friends so that I might have more of the community support and encouragement that I so needed.

Over time, my sense of failure at not always anticipating and attending to Naia's needs was replaced with a sense of awe at the amazing person that was my daughter. She is an entirely unique being, separate from me and from her father, and as such is sensitive to and able to articulate whether her own needs are being met. Indeed she challenges me to clarify for myself and for others what my needs are as opposed to my desires; Naia's insight into her own self and her relationship with others has granted me insight into the nature of my own relationship with her and with those closest to me. As a result, at present though neither she, nor her sister, dictate how family decisions are made or what the family priorities are, Bobby and I try to preserve their voices as valued and distinct within our family, carefully testing them against our own.

Parents who are learning with and from their child(ren), such as I am, will inevitably require affirmation of what they have learned about their mothering or fathering roles and responsibilities in order to feel as though their knowledge is valid and socially acceptable (Sheedy Kurcinka 1998, p. 2). Boreen and Niday (2000) portray learning relationships as pairings that provide supported dialogue, in the form of "the two-way exchange of listening and questioning" (pp. 2-3). Both in parent-child relationships and in mentorships with other parents, *learners can practice, adapt, and gain affirmation*: the knowledge "recognition" which Butler identifies (2004, p. 32). As such, Boreen and Niday (2000) affirm the goal of these learning partnerships to be the erasure of isolation and self-doubt (p. 2-3).

I am fortunate that I have developed such a relationship with our family's former nanny, Dopé. Her sense of humour and perspective has helped me to realize that I can laugh at myself and at the foibles that characterize some of my interactions with my daughters. Rather than take myself, or my understanding of external expectations, too seriously, Dopé's insight has helped to affirm me in my role as a mother learner rather than mother expert.

By engaging in a "culture of learning", *learner-members can develop a collective set of complex yet adaptable symbols which function as strategies that reflect their joint values* (Hansman 2001, p. 46-48; Wilson 1993, p. 77). This theory of *situated cognition*, devised by Arthur L. Wilson, was built on Vygotsky's socio-cultural learning research that highlighted the centrality of context and interaction in the learning of any activity (Hansman 2001, p. 44).

Through personal commitment and a sharing of resources, learners can negotiate the terms of their learning relationships. For example, novice learners and mentors can collaborate on *cognitive apprenticeships* that allow the novices to test and refine their knowledge, methods, and application, while also admiring and inquiring as to how their elders gained such "mastery" in their area of interest (Hansman 2001, p. 44-45). Subsequently, the novice must initiate new learning opportunities through which they can *adapt their skills and nourish the collective wisdom* so that they may contribute to a true "community of practice" (Wilson 1993, p. 77).

Parents engaged in informal learning interactions with their children and their mentors can accumulate their own knowledge by choosing alternative learning sites and relationships, establishing and claiming their identities as parents, and, articulating critiques of the identities and practices of parents legitimized by the established

52

discourses. Through a dialectical process of practice, reflection, refining, critical analysis, synthesis, and declaration, parents can move forward from insecurity to knowing, from uncertainty to affirmation in a "dynamic" learning process (Wilson 1993, p. 75-77; Olssen 1999, p. 142).

The messiness of interpersonal relationships has caused me to question the smoothness evident in popular discourses, an assumption that belies their constructed nature (Davis et al 2000, p. 211, Kinser 2008b, p. 123). These discourses oversimplify family interactions and divest them of their diversity and complexity, often portraying them as either entirely successful or unsuccessful. The limitations of expert parenting discourses have developed my resolve and increased my resistance, enabling me to empathize with "the art of not being governed like that and at that cost" (Foucault 1984a, p. 29).

Armed with this conviction I attempt to strip away normative judgments in my own mothering practices and perspectives. Adopting a learning attitude, I am living out a philosophy that tests my skills and strategies in daily interactions with my husband, my children, and other parents. Discerning which choices and patterns are optimal, Bobby and I together determine and assess our own barometer of *success* or *failure* according to our own terms and conditions and in doing so seek to affirm other parents practicing this critical parent-learning model (Marotta 2008, p. 205).

I believe it is my role as an educator to facilitate the development of critical awareness in other parents and to challenge them to view the sorrow, joy, anger, hope and weariness that define mothering and fathering as the experiences which shape us and teach us about our own limitations and needs, and the resources that we and our children seek. Together, our family relationships, as well as our mothering and fathering knowledge, practices, and identities can develop into an *art*, rather than the consumption and adoption of prescriptive parenting discourses that silence insights and undermine communal learning. Together we mother and father learners can join Fiona Green (2004) in reclaiming mothering and fathering through "conscious decisions and acts of dissidence" that resist the motherhood model and re-envision hopeful parent learning possibilities (p. 36).

I Labour

I straddle the road between
ostracism and belonging
selfhood and anonymity
individuality and community
connection and distinction
difference and sameness
membership and exclusivity.

each thought,
each word,
each action
commits me:
who chooses for me?

Community

Our culture depicts mothering as the key to female societal engagement. Mothers and non-mothers, just like *good* mothers and *bad* mothers, are seen in black and white, as stark opposites (Hays 1998 p. 125, 168; Ladd-Taylor & Umansky 1998, pp. 2-4; Ehreneich & English 2005, p. 357-358). However, as mother learners we occupy the grey area between these zones, regularly tying our variously complex families to the world and to the home while facilitating each of our passages to and from and in between. I am learning to discern where *good* and *bad* mothering merge and conflict in the mother learning process and am seeking to unsettle these binaries in order to alert others to the contradictions contained within these encounters. I am challenging myself and my community of learners to let go of our expectations for perfection that imply we ought to expect more of ourselves and of our families (O'Reilly 2006, p. 14; Timson 2010, p. 2). Instead I propose that we can risk standing out by virtue of our willingness to name the brokenness in ourselves, our families, and our societies, not out of a desire to apportion blame or to wallow in self-pity, but to create new possibilities for change (Nouwen 1990, 93; Palmer 2008, p. 135).

On the School Stage

Imagined all legs and arms, one eye
I feel a reject on Picasso's pile.
I gawk at fashion mavens braced

54

with false ideals of polish and lace;
their children turned out,
for committees they scout:
while wrestling we race for the doors and shout,
"what matters is not performance, and yet

I am jealous ..."[3]

... that you can let yours slip

... that you wear yours so well
you have forgotten it is a mask

... that you are better at your act
than I am at knowing when to reveal
the different sides of myself.

Is my mask slipping?
Am I ashamed,   lonely,   afraid,   joyful,   safe, or   proud?
I lay my masks aside,
and sigh.

Beyond the Motherhood Ideal

Patricia Hill Collins (1994) describes how the Caucasian, middle-class, and heterosexual ideal for North American families is comprised of two parents who split the responsibilities into "two oppositional spheres"—the 'female' caring role which "nurtur[es]" the family and the 'male' "economic" role which is concerned with providing for their material needs (p. 58). This gendered binary excludes non-females who seek to adopt a nurturing role.[4] In addition, this dominant model of motherhood asserts that work outside the home is solely a distraction from the primary home-based duties of mothering (Segura 1994, p. 212). Feminist thinkers, such as Fiona Green (2004), assert

---

[3] Spoken by the character, Billy Chenowith, to Ted Fairwell, Claire Fisher's new boyfriend in the 12th episode of season 5 of *Six Feet Under*. Billy's naked longing to be without his mental illness and its tendency to cripple his relationships is refreshing and also threatening at the same time. This kind of confession is a double-edged sword even in intimate relationships let alone polite social company or a professional setting.
[4] For an insightful and compassionate perspective on alternate gender possibilities and parenting listen to Kristin Nelson's radio documentary "The small person acquisition project" online.

that this is convincing evidence that this dominant model of motherhood is primarily a "site of women's oppression" (p. 31).

I have lived this familial ideal and know how far from perfect the reality is. While I have greatly benefited from the financial stability afforded our family by my husband's job as a physician, I have also resented his physical and emotional absence from our lives due to the enormous time and energy demands of his job. Simultaneously he has struggled with how best to support me while I care for our children physically, mentally, emotionally, psychologically and spiritually while also attending to the upkeep of our home.

At times our seemingly opposing family priorities have driven a deep wedge between us (Daly 2004). However, with time and a large quantity of both problem-solving and grace we have learned to see our roles as complementary. By viewing Bobby's work and presence with us as two aspects of his caring for our family, I have sought to move away from the polarizing extremes of the pervasive gendered discourse on parenting. Instead by discerning how his fathering integrates well with my mothering I have come to view him as my partner in this parent learning process. As evidenced by my personal example, the dominant motherhood model does not acknowledge the complexity of mothering, nor fathering, experience but provides a partial representation of mothers and fathers, as well as mothering and fathering practices (Chandler 1998, p. 273).

In an effort to learn about alternative models of mothering I began my certification training with the International Childbirth Education Association and a graduate program in adult education with Bobby's full support and encouragement. However, despite the many popular and academic resources available to me I struggled to find educational applications or academic theories that were able to reflect the simultaneously complex and dynamic, as well as predictable and monotonous, character of mothering and mother learning. Discouraged and wondering if I might have to abandon my efforts to lead and guide other mother learners, it was not until my second year of my studies that I began to understand that the specificities of intimate relations belie the narrowness of theoretical constraints while they also illustrate the "negotiations" we undertake to compromise with the external world, its demands, and its assumptions about mothering (Grumet 1988, p. 14-15).

On occasion, I am tempted to disappear into solitude because of my fear of being judged by external discourses and by those who adhere to their tenets (Grumet 1988, p. 93, 115, 78). Instead of trying to fit myself and my family into the artificial constraints on mothers and families I am reminded that I must also seek integrity in and through the relationships in which I am engaged by examining how I am implicated in the narratives of excluded mothers (Razack 1998, p. 45). Exhorted by the writings of critical educators, I am striving to resist the systems and the discourses that are used to exclude particular mothers from the larger mothering conversation. When I am disheartened by the conviction that I am complicit in silencing the stories and ignoring the example of marginalized mothers I examine my learning, practice and teaching, in order to foster change.

The systemic marginalization of mothers of colour that labels these women as *other*, as inferior mothers, has profoundly impacted my mother learning process. This racial discrimination against mothers of colour also ignores the "feminization of poverty" that drains many ethnic mothers of their limited resources and ignores their efforts to teach their children a vital and passionate sense of self in addition to the "survival" skills that they impart which many children of the dominant race and class lack (Mandell & Duffy 2005, p. 251; Hill Collins 1994, p. 68).

An exemplar of mother strength, our nanny, Dopé, has turned to her traditional African mothering patterns by seeking out "othermothers" (and otherfathers, on occasion), in a community of families who can support her in caring for her children while she works or studies (Grumet 1988, p. 162; O'Reilly 2006, p. 109-127). Rather than distinguishing between "those who are and are not like" her and inhibiting intimacy between her children and those who might love them, she sees the benefits of fostering new relationships for her children while caring for them through the work that she does outside of the home, as well as within it (Grumet 1998, p. 162; Hill Collins 1994, p. 164; O'Reilly 2006, p. 117).

Dopé's model of mothering seeks to be "dynamic and dialectical" rather than static and confining by emphasizing strength through community, flexibility, and diversity

(Lyon Jenkins 1998, p. 205). I honour Dopé for her leadership, inherited wisdom, resourcefulness, and creativity within the context of her family and communities for working outside of her home not out of personal choice, but for the benefit of both of our families (Chandler 1998, p. 271, 274; Hill Collins 1994, p. 67; hooks 1990, p. 48). Her example reinvigorates the dominant North American ideals that profess the right to pursue individual accomplishment and personal success with an integrity that far exceeds their constraints.

Building on the legacy of her fellow African-American mothers, Patricia Hill Collins (1994) renamed *motherhood* itself by re-envisioning *motherwork* as an inspiring counter-discourse:

> I use the term motherwork to soften the dichotomies in feminist theorizing about motherhood that posit rigid distinctions between private and public, family and work, the individual and the collective, identity as individual autonomy and identity growing from the collective self-determination of one's group. Racial ethnic women's mothering and work experiences occur at the boundaries demarking these dualities. (p. 59)

This passionate desire of mothers of colour to overturn the isolation and denigration of mothering itself recognizes that mother "work" is central to the health and well being of, not only the family but also, the community at large (Moraga 1997, p. 113).

Nevertheless, I do not believe that concerned parents can do this by simply ignoring the existence of predominant parenting discourses (Daly 2004, unpaginated, Conclusion). Rather, those of us with the "cultural capital" to resist these dominant discourses can challenge the idea that only a few are suitable to mother and father our children (Bordieu & Passeron 1973, p. 8). In order to resist short-term satisfaction, we must learn to "listen" for dissonance and seek opportunities to effect change and foster growth (Grumet 1988, p. 30). We must seize the privilege of "creat[ing] livable space", not just in our own home, but in the homes of those who do not have the privileges that we have, and in our communities at large (Rich 1986, p. 247).

I am challenged by Dopé to move beyond guilt at leaving my children with her, and with other caregivers; slowly I am learning to embrace her caring for my daughters as one aspect of my own caring for them. I am deeply grateful for her care for our children; through "wildly or tentatively, desperately, ambivalently, or tenderly" loving our children she has brought all four of us joy and blessing (Tuley 2008; p. 162). I hope that

I can express my gratitude for her presence and engagement with our children by also acknowledging how crucial her support of me has been in facilitating both expression of my "creative energies and desire" and in enabling me to establish a legacy of mother learning and knowing for myself and other mothers (Green 2008, p. 174). As a personal response, I am learning how to care for her and her children through listening, caring, and providing practical supports, as opportunities arise.

I hope that in this model of the home and the community, families find sanctuary for their weary hearts and spirits, while also learning how to develop a "critical consciousness" (hooks 1990, p. 41. 47; Mercado-Lopez 2008, p. 73-78) As teachers of strategic "resistance" together, I hope that Dopé and I are naming and seizing opportunities for personal and community change (p. 43).

Dopé and mother of colour scholars have challenged me to inquire as to how my mothering and teaching philosophies, relationships, and practices model resistance to oppression, suggest "strategies for survival", and provide a forum for various "narrative framings" and "modes of telling" (Thompson 1998, p. 530; Grumet 1988, p. 541-542). However, I am only slowly learning how to support Dopé, and her children, to overcome the dominance of the North American motherhood model through not just words, but also acts of resistance and care.

Relationship

> I've always longed for something else in my relationships—something woman-centred, something cross-generational, something extended, something sensual. (Moraga 1997, p. 18)

I must discern not only how to relate to my own children daily, but how to do so perceptively, while also exploring and managing my many other roles, identities, and relationships with the people and systems with which I interact (Kinser 2008b, p. 124). By abandoning my expectations of the persons who I assumed I, my children, Bobby, my parents, and others, were and adopting new, fluid understandings of who we desire ourselves to be, I am able to reinterpret these people, and the relationships in which I engaged in with them, dynamically and compassionately, a theme that I explore further in this section.

Mentors: From Whence She Comes ...

When reflecting on my maternal grandpa's influence in my life, I realized that he had been a model of integrity and playfulness whose presence was a source of stability for me and for my siblings. However, I recognize that as a grandfather his role was not that of an ongoing caregiver or disciplinarian, and therefore was much less demanding than those of my other family role models. Despite this, my grandpa's choice of gentleness was notable in his interactions with me, and my brothers, causing me to seek out his companionship and wise instruction regularly until his death when I was 14 years old. Now, as an adult, I have come to appreciate his gift for writing prose and poetry in a whole new light.

In memory of G. Fred Hamilton, my maternal grandpa. It is we who are truly blessed to have known you. We miss you and long to see you again.

Beloved

Remembered:
Patient faith
Expressing fervent hope.

Rare,
Humble righteousness
Belied immense strength.

Redeemed
In the wisdom of love …
Never failing.

Blessed

In contrast to my grandpa, as a child I perceived my maternal grandma as critical for constantly telling me to be more industrious and to adopt more hobbies. I felt as though she was implying that I was lazy because of my preoccupation with books and imaginative play. I now wonder whether her criticisms were based upon the lack of results I produced to account for my spare time.

As a younger woman I marveled at the way in which my grandma embraced her solitary roles of wife and mother while her husband was based in multiple foreign locales. Her conviction that she was both chosen and blessed in her vocation as a mother inspired both personal and public esteem in those around her. To this day I wonder how she elicited such regard in her era and community, when I suspect that indifference is more likely to be my primary reward should I choose a similar life path.

It was not until my grandfather's death that I began to get to know my grandmother on a personal level. As I continued to spend time with her either alone or with my mother I realized that she had much more humility, courage, and insight than I had previously observed. Our love for one another was celebrated in our differences and similarities rather than in emphasizing the distance between us; this complex relationship inspired me to invest in family over the long term.

The Junction

Ambling footpath
meandering over hills
and tumbling under dales

The traveler awed by crashing surf
and stung by biting wind
seeks pause

and is rewarded with peace

Bracken and wood
dragged by thorn
and torn by branch

The cathedral of steady spires
sends hope shivering and longing
for adventure and courage
as yet unexplored

Reveling in ardour
and enduring through revelation
each trace their map
towards memory of
the Way

Endeavouring to honour the example of mothering given to me by my own mother, I habitually buried my misgivings until the time when I was able to reflect on her particular model of maternity. I was and continue to be challenged by her stoic acceptance of the multiple domestic burdens she bore which belied her intellect and expertise as a physician; from manual labour and gourmet meal prep, to conflict resolution and accounting, my mom adeptly completed all of these familial responsibilities and bravely took on more each day. The self-denial that my mom practiced, both in her marriage and her parenting, caused her seemingly to disappear at times, and become unreachable in my mind's eye. I am so grateful that this process of articulating my mother learning has diminished my fears that I will not be able to measure up to my mom's example since I now know that she shares my longing for insight, love, and understanding into her life role and choices.

Ma in Memory and Grandma in Longing

With time that passes,
I too wait with ready arms
anticipating embrace;
I know the comfort that comes each time
with holding each one so tenderly
is stretching farther and further between.

As I saw you …

I recall being held in comfortable peace,
knowing I was where I belonged,
where I was loved.

I wonder how you go so long
without your child's embrace,
and I wish that I could wrap
my legs and arms about you now,
not for myself,
but for your longing
and for your heart of grace.

Eventually I began to reflect on how my father's example had influenced my mothering perspective and practices too. As I watch both my first and second daughters grow, I find myself wrestling with the legacy of impatience and anger passed on to me by him, and wonder when and if these responses were and are justified or self-serving. It is only with time and experience that I have come to conclude that the line is often more indistinct than I had previously realized. I have begun to understand that my dad's high expectations for himself and his children have caused him a lot of guilt and his children much anxiety. While he has been trapped by this legacy from his own father, where he is both victim and perpetrator, I have wondered how much he has sought to deny the tragedy of this pattern. While I strive to resist this polarized self-perception, I am uncertain if I am winning the battle, particularly when I sense self-doubt and anxiety beginning to creep back into my life.

This Anger: A Paternal Legacy

First his? Then yours. Now theirs. And mine.

It can burn low then flash.
Sometimes it lays waste to what is in its path.
Other times it lies dormant only to explode.

Did it flash and sear you, its flame maiming you?
Have you been scalded or did it turn you to ash?
Are you a column of stone?

I was only singed, but I fear that they were branded.
They do not reach out. You have started. I must.
Yet heal everyone, I cannot.

And so, I pray.

With Gratitude

The cost of both of my parents' polarized styles was evident to me in the context of my siblings' and my own adult relationships with our parents; the many things which remain unsaid and unresolved either cause us to continue to tiptoe around one another or to remain locked in tension and conflict. If only I might seek to nurture the best in my children without demanding too much of, or denying myself in the process, … but I am convinced that this is not merely a matter of hope nor finesse, but is borne of much time, patience and honest confession. These writings and the dialogue that it has prompted between me, my family and my friends have already begun to redeem the wounds that we have borne. I am so grateful for the many and varied insights granted to me through this mother learning process.

Despite my misgivings about their individual patterns, I know that each of my familial role models have granted me legacies that I cherish and am determined to pass along to my children: from my grandpa's resolve to share his knowledge and live with integrity, through my dad's strong sense of vocation and love of the written word, to my grandma's honesty and sense of humour, and finally, my mom's constancy of presence and passion for ideas. Somehow I hope that I might discern a way through these contrasts to a path that will build upon each person's strengths and enable me to learn from their particular shortcomings.

To My Godparents

It's so hard to be far away, to be unable to be living each day in your treasured company. I long to be in your presence, to be able to cherish each moment of wisdom, to gratefully relinquish my grip on fear, and to share in the hope that each morning brings. I long for my children to be certain of your encouragement and gentleness, to be witness to your steadfastness and pursuit of justice, to chuckle at your irreverence, and to celebrate with you in joy. I grieve that the opportunities for this are limited by both space and time, for you have touched me more than you will ever know. I wish that I would never have to let you go. And yet I know that this too is a lesson in which you are leading me and I am forever grateful for you both.

Godpappy,

On this your 81st birthday, I am grieving terribly right now, I feel as though I am doing nothing, so very far from you, while you are slipping away. I have so much to thank you for and it feels like so little time in which to say it.

I know that we have never spoken like this, but I want to take this occasion to celebrate that you are, and have been for me the spiritual father God gave me. I know that you are far from perfect, but I am so very grateful for how you taught me that grace could redeem us if we seek to live in spite of the guilt and shame which we know.

Your example, along with Godnanny's, Mom's, and Bobby's, has rooted me firmly in an empathic and compassionate faith that is hopeful and living. Through the ups and downs of your own life you were so present to me, never failing to encourage me and believe in me, far more than I ever could have done. You even inspired me to believe that I might grasp the intricacies of chemistry one day if I just put my mind to it!

I don't want to let you go. I don't want my children, my husband, and especially your wife, your children, your grandchildren, and my mom to be without you. And yet I don't want you to suffer. But these things are not my choices to make, just as they are not yours either.

My choice is to thank you, and to thank God for you: for you sharing your love, your playfulness, and your incisive mind with me.
With much love, Fiona

Seeking Family Support

My father was the first person to inquire of me whether I might be experiencing Post Partum Depression (PPD) and to encourage me to seek medical support and counseling. I have often wondered why he was the first to approach me about this and now know that he was able to see me as he would another of his patients (for he was trained as a family physician) rather than just as his daughter. Having lived apart since I was approximately 10 years old, he has told me that he did not experience the emotional confusion of seeing his daughter in pain, but rather could readily empathize with my situation. His personal insight into his own diagnosis with depression also assisted him in articulating that there was no shame in needing medical or personal help, but rather hope and opportunity for both my marriage and my family.

Despite the fact that my mother had not planned on coming, I was very glad that she came to be with me and care for me when I asked her to upon Bobby's return to work. Having not invited her in the beginning she had not come earlier, since she did not want to impose herself upon Bobby and me or interfere with the intimacy of our bonding as a new family. In this case, it was my ignorance that had caused me not to ask for help, however, I believe that in the long term it was my own shame and sense of failure as a mother perpetuated by the dominant discourse on motherhood that presented the most significant obstacle to my opening up to my family (Green 2004; Segura 1994; Smith 1987; Hill Collins 1994; Stadlen 2004).

The legacy of mothering children without a physically present father early on erroneously caused me to believe that I ought to be capable of mothering on my own as well. Afraid of exposing myself as an unfit mother by asking for advice and assistance repeatedly, I did not reach out to anyone for months, even Bobby. During the first year of becoming a mother it was only when I could suspend this fear long enough to grab a hold of a rare offer of support that I found respite and a promise of hope in mothering.

However, I now know that both my mother's and grandmother's experiences of caring for their children were vastly different despite the fact that both of their husbands were not at their sides parenting the children day in and day out. For instance, while my grandfather worked in many countries while my grandmother, my mom, and my uncle remained in England, he and my grandmother wrote daily of their circumstances and shared virtually all decisions regarding the nurturing of their two children. In contrast, my mom and dad regularly differed on how to raise my brothers and me, another cause of strife for them.

Although I had initially assumed that I could handle taking care of a new baby by myself after Bobby's return to work, four days postpartum I was suffering from extreme sleep deprivation, difficulty nursing, and a resulting disorientation and confusion. Distraught, I was panicking over Naia's neediness and my inability to cope, and fearful about Bobby's frustration with both the situation and with me. Exhausted by his efforts to provide financial stability for our family and live up to the high standards of residency training, Bobby was absent from our home for up to fourteen hours a day during that period. His being so physically removed from the daily tasks of caring for Naia made it difficult for us to relate to one another's roles and responsibilities.

This sense of being overwhelmed negatively influenced my other family relationships as well. Though my mother helped me to survive the crisis of Naia's first 2 weeks at home, I did not recognize that I could have used the opportunity to learn from her knowledge and experience about how to care for myself and for a newborn baby. Having been trained as a pediatrician and raised 3 children of her own, she was an invaluable resource that I neglected to invest in at that time. Thank goodness I now acknowledge the extreme pressure I was under physically, emotionally, psychologically, and spiritually. For the first time in my life, I felt unable to turn to anyone for help, despite the fact that I had many resources around me since I could not see the opportunity for grace to intervene, but only how I must strive to be the *perfect* mother who must innately know everything and turn to no one for help.

As the depth of these challenges began to surface my mom's worries about me increased but she was reluctant to approach me with her suspicions. In order to not undermine any confidence I might have gained she approached Bobby with her concerns. However, since now I was accomplished at hiding my confusion and discouragement from Bobby he was convinced that I was managing better and dissuaded her from questioning me at that time.

Upon my mom's return to Ontario, I was only just beginning to grasp the depth of work involved in caring for Naia, but building on the little that I did glean from her I had confirmed that Naia was extremely perceptive, strongly bonded to me, and highly sensitive to stimuli. What I didn't recognize in the short term was that I would continue to perceive her to be very demanding for some time and that her personality would require me to discern: a) what her expectations of me were; b) whether I could and would fulfill these expectations; and, c) how I would respond to her, her sister, their dad, and myself, when I could not or would not fulfill what I perceived to be their expectations. My desire to never fail others, especially my family, often caused me to neglect my own needs, further exacerbating my isolation and my anxieties, but would eventually force me to reach outside of my family for anonymous help and support.

Pantomime

Why are we so fearful of intimacy,
of touch, and of memory ...
for it is all that is golden?

From the caress of the hands
to the dancing of the eyes,
our stories are the sum of our togetherness,
our trust, our distances, and our absences.

We cannot count the cost
by measuring our apologies
nor our shame,
by our frailty or our loss.

Why avert the gaze
or descend into the shadows?

Our hiding places are built
of straw and sawdust:
though layered and intricate
they succumb
to the most minor of intrusions
and reveal us as longing
for what we deny.

Regret: A trilogy at nighttime

What follows is a three-part lament for the length of time it takes me to recognize the mother-learning moments, often due to the variety of complex and, at times, contradictory emotions that come with being a parent, particularly one who has at least one child with a sensitive temperament. During and after these moments, the visceral connection that I have with my daughters can take me by surprise. While momentarily, my passions may paralyze me, I am so grateful that I can still be shaken into seeing those around me with new, more compassionate eyes.

A Keening

No gentleness discerned in infant sleep,

nor tenderness in our unions.
We're apt to gnawing, nonsense pride,
and confuse-ed lamentation.
Bind not your foment,
weep instead,
wrath loosed pleads
com-passion.
Stifle not your lonely cries,
but pity me
shaken,
still,
and smote in adoration.

Breathing Icicles

droplets stored
as pattern and scheme
suspended in silent conversation
blended in rhythm of mistaken identity
released as a torrent

catch and borrow
phrases for
the basement of the universe

Longing

Tears are
lemon-drained yellow in the sunlight
from pain
and my hand kneads my belly
as if you were here

Someday
I will knot a coil for you
that will not slip or bind
but lengthen
beyond the hours
of lemon-stained sunlight

Embodiment

> I am really asking whether women cannot begin, at last, to *think*
> *through the body*, ... I know no woman ... for whom her body is not a
> fundamental problem: its clouded meaning, its fertility, its desire, its
> so-called frigidity, its bloody speech, its silences, its changes and
> mutilations, its rapes and ripenings. There is for the first time today a
> possibility of converting our physicality into both knowledge and power.
> (italics in original) (Rich 1986, p. 284)

Mapping Out My Story: Living the Learning

I was still in a haze from labour and delivery when I began to realize that I was not only expected to be fully responsible for this tiny, vulnerable child, but also to know innately how to mother her. The day nurse in the maternity ward spent more of her time chatting with me about her own life than showing me how to care for my Naia, lulling me into believing that someone else would be enlisted to take care of her, at least for the short term.

Yet, when later that first day the night nurse arrived, I was dismayed to find out that, in what had believed was my ignorance but I now know was the haze of childbirth, I had not performed any of the expected cataloguing of my child's changes or feeds or even taken any of the pain medications provided for me. Even though the night nurse tried to reassure me that it was the day nurse's job to clarify the importance of these tasks, I felt that I was a complete fool for not intuiting them as priorities. From that point onward, my confusion and shame also interfered with my ability to trust my day nurse and ask for her assistance with any of my concerns. Based on observations of the mothers that I knew I had an internal conviction that I ought to know how to care for my own child without requiring outside help, therefore when I did not know how to articulate my lack of knowledge and my worries I felt very inadequate. When the hospital had me secure Naia in her new car seat and ready my bags for departure, the sinking feeling in my stomach deepened: they were going to let me take her home.

Initially I turned to Naia to teach me how to be a mother, since I understood her to be responsible for this change in my identity. I hoped that she would reveal a complete strategy for caring for her needs within a matter of days. Thus, imagine my surprise when, though she arrived weighing only 6 pounds and quite scrawny at birth, she declared herself as a force with which to be reckoned and right from the beginning was determined to get everything that she wanted. Whether it was milk, comfort, attention, or anything else her heart desired, she seemed relentless and unconcerned for whether her needs were reasonable--imagine that! She was very active--this being evident even in the womb, where it felt as though she were swimming laps both day and night--as well as very vocal, expressing what appeared to be anger, frustration, or impatience, virtually without ceasing.

Mentally scattered by exhaustion, and without any confidence in my abilities, I briefly shifted my attentions to the community health nurse who patiently attended to me during the first week. Her charm, encouragement, and self-deprecating humour were the brightest lights available to me during a very frightening period leading me to conclude that somehow she must hold the answer to how I would bridge myself from uncertainty towards clarity. Sadly her support was limited by the constraints of her schedule and I felt unworthy to request that she provide me with additional support once my mother arrived to help me. Once I knew that she was not going to be with me I feverishly began to record any and every morsel of advice she offered on a mountain of post-it notes which I affixed to the walls of both Naia's and my bedrooms.

Although Bobby and I were intimidated by the passion which defined Naia's cries and with how easily stimulated she was by light, movement, colour, noise, temperature, and even the emotions of others, it never occurred to us at the time that we were struggling with the shock of being confronted with a strong personality seemingly so unlike each of our own. We wrestled not with whether we loved her, which neither of us ever doubted, but with whether we could relate to her, and I was plagued by the belief that I was incapable of bearing the responsibility for her care and her well being regardless of whether Bobby was present or not. This seemed to me to be the only priority of motherhood--Naia's well being--and for the first 4 to 6 months, little led me to believe otherwise.

My fears that I was somehow a failure as a mother, unwilling and/or unable to provide for all her needs and desires as she moved seamlessly between inconsolable anguish and rage, only ceased when she was fed and held. For these brief moments she was peaceful and adoring, granting me a lifeline that I tightly grasped deep inside of

71

myself. Unfortunately, my anxieties and insecurities drove a wedge between Bobby and myself and caused him to occupy himself more with his work of caring for his patients and studying for his exams, while I retreated into myself, ashamed of my self-doubts and disturbed by our mostly unsettled child. I often asked myself the following questions: what is wrong with me or what does everyone else here know about how to be a successful mother that I don't?

Even when I first began seeing my psychiatrist at the Reproductive Mental Health program in Women's Hospital I could not move beyond seeing my depression as the "shameful illness" of which Jean Vanier (2001) speaks (p. 33). He clarifies that many depressed and anxious people in our culture respond as I did by spending most of my time and energy fixating on my negative feelings about myself and about my relationship with Naia and yet hiding this doom and gloom from others out of a fear of being judged as a crazy person and, in this case, as an unfit mother (p. 35-37).

Gradually, with the patient listening ear of my psychiatrist, psychologist, and fellow mothers wrestling with depression, I began to view myself as "normal and natural" in my negative response to my mothering experience and that I was worthy of "compassion" for my struggle to once again restore hope to my mothering "story" (p. 37, 33). Unfortunately, I did not fully embrace my response as hopeful until one of my academic committee members told me that she saw my response to my circumstances as a mother as "a spirited and intelligent response" (Gleason, in conversation, December 16th, 2009.)

The Jury's Still Out ...

Disciplining the body
that nurtured a child,
found me wandering alone
rhythm and melody gone wild.
From wretchedness to resilience
I have learned the capriciousness of control,
in agony and anxiety,
and with uncertain goals.
Knowing now the hope that healing required,
with humility and hormones
(help undisguised),
I grieve for the losses due to fear and denial,

and strike out with conviction and humour:
... on trial.

Breastfeeding as a Measure of a *Good* Mother ...

> A 2005 study out of Kent University found that how women feed their
> babies have become a measure of motherhood. The thinking out there
> is that mothers have a responsibility to breastfeed, no matter what ...
> at all costs. (Helfenbaum 2009, p. 8-9)

When I began attending the drop-in sessions at the community health centre, for fear of being repudiated for making irrelevant inquiries, I phrased my queries to target only how I might achieve a certain benchmark in Naia's development rather than how I might understand and respond to her needs in order to strengthen our relationship. Surprisingly, none of the many nurses present ever questioned my prolonged search for such arbitrarily imposed knowledge rather they reinforced my belief that health care professionals were almost exclusively concerned with the production and maintenance of a healthy child. Regularly the nurses espoused the La Leche mantra that "the child" is the authority on what they need, while denying or ignoring whether that approach is beneficial or even tenable for the whole family, both individually and collectively (including the mother, the father, additional siblings, and additional caregivers) (Leach 1997, p. 57).

These women (for invariably they were) never questioned my generic search for knowledge, despite the fact that this searching for averages rather than specifics was a vicious cycle that perpetuated my sense of inadequacy and failure. They insisted that I adhere to the process of demand feeding rather than adopting a schedule, even though Naia was gaining weight in leaps and bounds and I was wasting away, both in terms of my weight and my ability to maintain any sense of proportion on a daily basis. The nurses never inquired how I was managing to feed her at that rate and not face complete exhaustion (I must have looked so good, they never suspected!). Instead they fostered my near obsession with whether or not Naia was getting enough milk despite all of the signs affirming this, thereby reinforcing the message that her physical well being was of paramount importance.

No one encouraged me to stay at the health centre when, within 15 to 20 minutes of my arrival, Naia would become inconsolable. Since I could not bear the looks of worry, pity, consternation, annoyance, or distraction which I received from the other mothers, the guest speakers, and the nurses I packed us both up to go. Not one person would offer to hold my child for me to give me a break, nor would they empathize with me about Naia's temperament--she would never lie on her back or belly and coo or kick her feet alongside the 10-20 other babies there—no one inquired whether I was managing the strain which I was sure was written all over my face and body.

> We need to take into consideration what's going on in a mother's life, and help her make the best decision she can.... it's important that we respect each other's decisions as women and as mothers.... I wonder if we're creating breastfeeding trauma by insisting women nurse for whatever time we've decided is normal. (Helfenbaum 2009, p. 9)

Learning to take care of my health

Before I had children I thought that my health was my concern alone, but what I have begun to learn is that when my health and my quality of life suffer, so do my relationships. At first I tend to wallow in self-pity, grumbling along while I pretend that I am bearing up under the discomfort. However, once I am unable to sleep and my ability to engage in physical activity or get outside is affected I begin to lash out at others in frustration. In the beginning I can delude myself into believing that I am simply having a bad day, or a rough week at worst, but when I have absolutely no patience left for my sick children, for their lack of cooperation and enthusiasm, and no sense of humour in hindsight, I know that I am losing all sense of perspective. As I slip into despair and become more and more negative towards Bobby and/or the kids, I am forced to recognize that the status quo is not tenable anymore and I must start to look for ways to restore myself to health.

For example, in the past I gladly took pain medication to counteract flare-ups in my back. However, as I have aged and my activity level has become more inconsistent, I have not been able to bounce back from these periods of limited activity and discomfort. This finally became a problem at the end of winter and during the early spring of 2009 when I was determined to use my bike as my main means of transportation despite my limited time and energy. I was convinced that this would allow me to remain physically fit, while also saving the environment and not competing with my school, work, and family demands. Once again, my efforts to live up to the expectations espoused by the public discourses on *good* mothering and *good* citizenship were leading me down a very treacherous path.

Inevitably this meant that I would have to use my bike and trailer to transport myself, my younger daughter, and, at times my elder daughter, to and from school. Even at the peak of my resolve I was doing this no more than 3 times a week both ways. Only twice weekly was a big improvement on my previous habits and the benefits were many: I was getting exercise; we were all getting lots more fresh air; there were fewer battles over getting Anica into the car seat (even though we sometimes had the same battle over getting her into the trailer seat); and, we all tended to be happier during the process. Anica regularly sang songs en route, Naia enjoyed her book or developed her skills biking on the road, and I was getting into fewer driver altercations: ensuring that we were more at peace with one another and I was able to focus more on my work demands for the rest of the morning.

Sadly, this was not to last. I only made it until April before my back and/or hips began to protest. Naively I hoped I would be back on the bike if I just swam and stretched a little more regularly and eased off a bit on the biking. However, it didn't take long before I was unable to swim at all and was at my doctor's office trying to figure out if there was a more chronic problem to address. Eventually I could hardly do anything without being in agony. To stand at the counter preparing a meal, to sit at the dinner table to eat, or to lift Anica were tasks that rendered me fully incapacitated.

Unfortunately, in contrast to when I was first diagnosed with scoliosis at 17 years of age, I received no definitive diagnosis as to why I was experiencing so much pain. My biking had now stopped completely and I was driving my girls to school and all of their activities, having to resort to a daily dose of painkillers to manage the pain that would persist for months.

Yet the student in me was dissatisfied with this solution. I could not reconcile myself to taking pain medication for the rest of my days even though I could justify taking my anti-depressants. Though the imbalance in hormones caused my depression I could not ignore attending to each of my many triggers: isolation, powerlessness, devaluation, and alienation. Similarly, I could see that the effects of my misaligned skeletal structure and diminished muscle strength and tone were all contributing factors, but I was not willing to concede to lifelong hip and back pain that necessitated the consistent use of medication unless I had exhausted all other forms of pain management.

In the short term, I began to rely more heavily on our nanny to care for our family through meal preparation and for engagement in outdoor activities with Naia and Anica. The increased pressure on our family income together with the added gasoline costs required for driving the girls to school and on various errands caused me concern while at the same time, I felt as though I was paying an employee to satisfy my whims and retreating into self-pity instead considering longer term solutions. Torn between my desire to be a *good* mother and a *good* environmental citizen I was unable to see how I was losing myself in these discursively created roles.

It was not until I read Jean Vanier's (2001) book, *Seeing beyond depression,* this past winter that I realized my response to my back/hip pain mirrored how my initial response to postpartum depression had been rooted in my dissatisfaction with my mothering role and relationships. Vanier echoed my psychiatrist's, and my academic committee's affirmation that my initial response of dismay and loss at the dramatic changes that I had experienced were completely valid. However, I needed for this acceptance to permeate more than my rational brain so that I could begin to understand my body's limitations, and heal, literally one step at a time.

Knowing now that it was not arthritis or the minor bone degeneration I have due to calcium loss that caused my pain, I was neither amused nor satisfied when my first physiotherapist told me that I did not need to know the cause of my pain. When I was able to do a minimal level of exercise and I was performing basic mothering tasks (while still taking pain killers) he was content for me to call him only if my pain returned to the level of the previous six months.

In the short term I remained dissatisfied, but after almost 4 months I began to discern the reasons for my unease. While doing independent research on different exercise approaches I was finally able to understand the reason for my concerns: namely, that I had received no encouragement from my physiotherapist to be resourceful and to attempt to restore health to myself, but only to manage my symptoms.

76

Thankfully, one month later I found a physiotherapist who began to teach me why my body was in pain and helped me to learn how I might begin to manage it without painkillers. By improving my core body strength through regular exercises I have begun to reduce my dependence on medication and am hopeful that if I put in the hard work and consistent effort, with support, I can strengthen myself and restore health to my body (and my mind) for the long term.[5]

Short Shrift

> I am in that mother's skin, ... knowing I could have been her. Still can.
> (Moraga 1997, p. 97)

Your body knowledge
and knowing feelings
live dormant in your mind's eye
until creative vision or sheer force of will
speaks, writes, or acts them into execution.
Now a game
is laid out for all to poke and pick apart,
like ravens with their gleaming eyes
cackling as they
plunder the treasures of your life.
Chase them away.

Doing Versus Being

When occupied with doing, with performing the mundane tasks that keep the family cared for, we mothers can lose ourselves in pursuit of the ideal of self-sacrifice. This process can also cause us to forget what connects us to one another, an ideal that is far more important than all of these particular details and their finite value. Conversely, mothering does not have to be defined as oppressive because it necessarily requires interdependence, so long as one's life goal is not to be "autonomous" from everyone else (Chandler 1998, p. 277).

---

[5] I must clarify that both 7 years ago and now I could not have begun to restore health to myself without my anti-depressants. I did try that and my ability to make very basic decisions was adversely affected. I was virtually paralyzed by guilt, fears, and anxiety that plagued me regularly. Worst of all, I almost completely lacked any sense of humour or hope. Instead with my resources bolstered by balancing my hormones, in both situations I was able to advocate for myself and seek treatment that did not make me submissive, but more empowered.

> 'Mother' is an identity formed through a repetition of practices which constitute one as so profoundly interconnected that one is not one, *but is simultaneously more and less than one.* (italics in original) (Chandler 1998, p. 274)

The Picture of a Healthy Educator

Moms aren't supposed to, aren't allowed to get sick. Unfortunately, I am a mom who becomes sick on a fairly regular basis.

I don't have a chronic or a life-threatening illness, I am simply vulnerable to what for most others is just a mild annoyance: the common cold. Since I have asthma, and a couple of regular, healthy young children who transport every virus and bacteria known to humankind in their travels to and fro, I simply cannot fight off every germ that comes my way. When I am healthy, my asthma doesn't limit my activities on a daily basis, but as soon as I am exposed to the kindergarten cough I am felled within a few short days.

Invariably, it settles into my lungs, producing a cough that drives my husband batty, disturbs our sleep, and seriously limits my energy level. At first, the car becomes our second home, even though guilt sets in as soon as I turn the key in the ignition at the beginning of the day.

I found myself feeling exceptionally ashamed when, on one occasion, I had forgotten that it was "bike to school week". Sadly, I didn't even manage to park in the video store parking lot around the corner from the school, as the cheat sheet (which the school distributed, perpetuating the responsible parenting discourse) had advised us parents to be certain to do. Instead I naively drove right up to the school and wondered out loud why there were so many parking spaces available. Only then did my precocious 5 year old declare that we ought to be sparing the environment "like everyone else was today".

My asthma aggravation peaks when it interferes with my ability to do my professional job. As a parent educator, it is hard to be taken very seriously when you can hardly breathe without hacking and wheezing, and it certainly doesn't endear you to new mothers and fathers when you are doing it in their infant's face. Many people believe that professionals must be present and prepared regardless of the cost, whereas learners may choose to risk or sacrifice their investment since it is only their

78

loss and no one else's. In my circumstances, the cost to me, to my family, and to my professional life is too great if I do not take care of myself, but is it greater if I am perceived to be inconsistent or unreliable by my students?

> I imagine curriculum ... that returns us to the sites of the body and of the emotional ... that embraces passion and emotion [and] can negotiate our lives as mothers and daughters and in all the multiple texts of women's embodied experience. (Dunlop 1998, p. 120-121)

Entering into the Mothering Dialogue through A/r/tography

In Madeleine Grumet's (1988) introduction to *Bitter Milk: Women and Teaching*, she challenges women to risk confessing our embodied experience of "nurturance" by using it to inform our individual learning and practice rather than allowing patriarchal systems to devalue the present and future impact of "reproductive" knowledge (p. xix; 6; see also Green 2008, p. 174, O'Reilly 2006, p. 11; Gore 2000, p. 42). Having felt stifled by both internal and external discourses on mothering and parenting, Grumet's (1988) exhortation to engage in, and learn from, the layers of identity revealed by mothering spoke to the artist, learner, and educator in me all at once (p. 67).

The Risk of Femininity and Embodiment

Grumet (1988) states that our mother nature is inherently compromised and contradictory, simultaneously "subjective" and "objective", and urges us not to hide behind our own discomfort with our emotions (p. 88, xix). Her claim is that "knowledge from and about the body is about the world" but that most of the time women "hide" their insights, their daily learning, and indeed, their very selves for fear of offending the taboos of respectable society (p. 29, 58). This resonated with my experience of being a mother who often strives to appear positive and engaged with the outside world while internally struggling with the many demands of motherhood and the expectation that I ought to excel at mothering and so much more (Gore 2000, p. 42-45, 74).

Our society exhorts us to resist meaningful relationships that might challenge our independent spirit while it feeds our yearning for sporadic, romantic encounters that provide us with temporary self-gratification (Grumet 1988, p. 98; Chandler 1998, p. 284). This discourse triggers guilt in me at my negative responses to my children, even though I know that it is unrealistic for me to seek only positive interactions with them, thereby avoiding the costs of intimacy that lie so close to the surface of my being (Green 2008, p. 172; Grumet 1988, p. 71-72).

As a new mother I felt profoundly violated by Naia's need for and expectations of me and imprisoned by what I perceived to be my shameful resistance to the role that I had chosen for myself (Grumet 1988, p. 106; O'Brien Hallstein 2008, p. 114). Despite having invested a lot of energy into my relationships with the members of my family of origin, at times I have wondered whether I wanted to put so much of myself and of my resources into a family of my own (even this far down this road). Unable to recognize myself, I wondered whether I had become a "stranger"; in my role of new mother as I wrestled with who I was and wasn't, and who I ought to be (Grumet 1988, p. 97-99).

Privilege and Possibility

The psychological toll that mothering takes on me has caused me, at times, to believe that I am being held together by a tenuous thread. This "choreography" of intimacy in which I engage with my daughters has forever marked me as reluctant and yet cherished, a conflict that both unsettles me and makes me want to dig deeper into the sources of my discontent (Grumet 1988, p. 98; Stadlen 2004; Green 2008). The raw emotions and the brute physicality of our mother-daughter encounters at times reduces me to my visceral self; I descend into agony and resentment, or avoidance of my mother-self (Jagger 1989; Rich 1986, p. 52). Despite my best efforts to conceal my vulnerability, my façade is shaken by the words and actions of those who have the power to ignore me one moment and claim me the next (Moraga 1997, p. 40).

I Am Dis-couraged

Your contrariness
drives me beyond distraction
to exasperation
and even fury;
held hostage
by your whims and wants,
I am frustrated by your
negative
inter
activity.
I fit-full-y
and
RESENT-full-y
(breathe)
attend to your basic
<u>needs</u>
for sleep, food, and attention.
I do not r-e-a-c-h out to you.
I am drawn into,
I with-draw.
I spar (#&!) with vengeful spite
and punish.
I am base and dis-respectful ...
lowering the bar,
and confounding myself.

                    Do not
         ~~~~ drown ~~~~~
          ~~~ in a sea of ~~~
MY EXPECTATIONS
         um
or j   p to ATTENTION!
like a dog doing tricks.
L
   o
    s
      i
       n
        g   sight
of your FUNDA-MENTAL needs
for en-courage-ment, connect--------tion,
and the pursuit of JOY
                           C
                       Y L
HOW DO I BREAK THIS C   E
so that we see an alternate <--- WAY:
an honouring of your trust,
a **strengthening** of your
Be-ing, and a LOVE-ing
which fosters new intimacies
each day.

My initial attempts to control the intimacy of my relationships with my children from leaking into other aspects of my life not only hindered the development of the bonds between me and my children, but it also diminished the role which my husband could play in each of our lives. Due to my narrow understanding of both mothering and fathering roles I could not grasp how "the father, the friends, [and] the world" could interact with me as a mother and with one another to "enrich and extend" our respective spheres rather than further alienate us from one another (Grumet 1988, p. 15). However, I slowly began to grasp that by inviting Bobby to share with me in caring for our children I might enrich each of the relationships that bound us together.

Since each of us have unique and creative ways of loving Naia and Anica, both girls have thrived on our multiple expressions of care and affirmation as they "receive and respond to our love" with deep gratitude and generosity (Grumet 1988, p. 178-179).

In addition I have discerned that my negative emotions are often underpinned by my insecurity in my mothering role and my fear of rejection, but I now claim the conviction that these emotions and responses need not be stifled in an effort to "sanitize the experience" of mothering, but may be an opportunity to bridge families through support and greater understanding (Tuley 2008, p. 163).

Though my "outlaw emotions" initially prompted me to isolate myself out of fear of social condemnation they later led me to seek out a community where I would not be deemed a *bad* mother for my feelings and reactions and my need to express them to others (Jagger 1989; Ladd-Taylor & Umansky 1998, p. 2; Gore 2000, p. 17, 220). At first I sought affirmation through the stories of other mother and father learners, but soon I realized that this distant contact with other parents was not a satisfactory solution (Aron, 2002; Sheedy Kurcinka 1998; Stadlen 2004; Sandborn 2007; Pruett 2001; Howard 2007; Iovine 2007; Limbo & Rich Wheeler 1986). Before long I came to understand that I needed to claim my own learning and have it affirmed by a community of peers before I could discern which knowledge I still wanted to acquire. As a result, I sought to build upon my mothering practice through a dynamic process of reflection and dialogue with other parents.

Learning to Mother, Learning to Teach, Teaching Mothers and Fathers

My search for a community of parent learners led me to many resource places. In order of my discovery of them, they were: a new spiritual home with a vibrant core of families who had a commitment to compassionate learning and action; a "Positive, Encouraging Parenting" (PEP) Program where constant affirmation, ideas, and resources provided a safe place for parents to ask questions and articulate their doubts; a postnatal education program and a Masters program in adult education where I might freely explore and challenge what the sources were for my mother discontent; and, a spiritual director to facilitate my integration of these many resources for mother learning and support.[6]

---

[6] PEP was planned and led by a psychologist in the Reproductive Mental Health Program, at Women's Hospital and Health Centre.

Both needy and needed, both "subject and object", I am learning to risk loving and mothering despite the perceived short term cost and suffering to me (Grumet 1988, p. 27). By truly loving I am risking a "wide embrace" that employs empathy, generosity, and encouragement rather than pretence, control, and/or jealousy (Grumet 1988, p. 179-180; Hewett 2008, p. 27-29).

Risk and hope are required to grant us insight into ourselves. They are also necessary to enable us to foster deeper trust between us adults, and between adults and the children for whom we care. As a result, I am striving to expand my definition of who can teach me about, and model for me, mothering my own children (Grumet 1988, p. 91, 97; Hewett 2008, p. 22. 27). In this way my personal "curriculum" mediates between my own, and my childrens', lived experiences and the world that constructs knowledge in and around us (Grumet 1988 pp. xvi-xviii; Davis & Sumara 1998, p. 83).

Broader Implications

Despite the disconnections so apparent in our daily interactions with others, being a mother learner has taught me to reclaim the truth that we are unquestionably interrelated, intimate with, and revealed by our families (Grumet 1988, p. 27; Chandler 1998). Grumet's argument that we should employ our mothering experience as a catalyst to inspire authentic descriptions of intimacy and labour that are intrinsic to both "teaching and nurturance" is at the root of my art (p. 91). As my confidence in my mothering and mother knowledge began to build and my resources to expand I saw how I might reach out to other mother and father learners with compassion and encouragement (O'Reilly 2006, p. 104). My work, both mothering and teaching, has become my passion: these "creative processes" cause me to risk judgment and dismissal, but they also invite engagement, affinity, and mutuality with others (Grumet 1988, p. 78; Hewett 2008, p. 27; O'Reilly 2006, p. 117, 124).

As a mother and wife, student and teacher, I have discovered a depth of "aesthetic" inspiration which went previously untapped (Grumet 1988, p. 88). By concurrently practicing the arts of mothering, marital dialogue, reflective writing, and parent mentoring, I have had my resolve to cherish my family restored through a combination of: communion, blessing, retreat, and affirmation (Smith 2000, p. 140). By grace, I hope I may continue to be nourished and healed even while learning and teaching others about the *art of learning to live* and *be* parents.

Compassionate Parenting

As I search for possibilities for learning and relating to those I love I realize that this risk requires of me many resources, including energy and ideas, in order to face the challenges that still lie ahead of me in mothering. I am making a daily, if not hourly recommitment to caring for each of my children rather than resenting their reliance on, and love for me. Using a combination of humour, humility, and gratitude to recognize that I am always being either tested and/or taught by my children, slowly I am gaining new insight into "the courage to be imperfect" (Dreikurs 1964, p. 38-54).

I have begun to employ empathy and compassion, rather than control and authority, in my efforts to learn how to be humble in relation to my children and other mother learners (Nouwen 1990, p. 65). Until I could move beyond the unreasonable expectations that I had for myself, expectations based on the assumptions that I could become a *good*, a *perfect*, mother, I could not move beyond risk into hope and new opportunity, nor could I trust that in this I would find a new insight into myself and other parent learners. This leap of faith required an emotional and psychological strength that I had previously not explored and a spiritual faith rooted in an understanding of grace that could only be described in artistic phrase and rhetorical musings.

Meditations On What a Mother Cannot Do ...

Courage:
if I could reap it, I would;
a rare commodity
granted only to those who grieve.

There is a weariness, an aging, a sorrow
close to the surface of the eyes
that I would spare you;
I would move mountains if I could.

However, I need not slay your dragons
nor mince my words until they contain no meaning,
but may I open my eyes,
shadow their steps,

and defend your insight,
honouring your way.

Innocence lost
yet wisdom gained,
for which your soul will be richer
I pray.

Truth in Restraint

There is such beauty and joy in a child's person: in their sincerity and their laughter and in their abandonment to the moment without pretension or self-consciousness. In the face of such innocence when do we broach the truths that make us uncomfortable? We cannot protect our children from these truths, but when is the right time to share them? How do we explain that during the times when loving, when even just being, is difficult it will still be worth every moment? I am beginning to learn that parenting is not about leaping in and simply offering up false promises or reassurances, but rather about holding back and holding onto our desires. By denying ourselves what *we* want in the short term and learning to watch, to see, to listen, to hear, to walk with our children as they approach and experience each different situation we are offering up the best of ourselves and of our hope *for them* (Palmer 2008, p. 114-115, 129; Nouwen 1990, p. 69).

Cherish: A Song of Knowing

Spread over your face is a mischievous grin,
while your watchful eyes take it all in.
Muscles coiled and ready to spring,
thoughtfully choosing the moment and then, with absolute trust and startling grace
you launch yourself smoothly
in-to my embrace

A love of performance and a passionate drive,
insatiable curiosity and the ability to surprise,
your lust for life,
and compassion for others,
confounds me,
inspires me,
mysterious child.

Daily you teach me of vulnerability and desire,
you stretch me
and guide me
in the cacophony and quiet.

You provide the soundtrack to my days
and my nights;
my patience tested,
my creativity alight.
How can I thank you for all that you are?

Faith

The spiritual insights that I have gained since becoming a mother have become a essential aspects of my mother learning process. Elizabeth Tisdell (2008) clarifies that when *spirituality* and *religion* are adapted from nouns to adjectives, to that which is *spiritual* and *religious*, their meanings become synonymous with one another: both describe an individual's or a community's "experience or imaginative work" merging with their understanding of the sacred and the mundane (p. 29-30). This process is described as being a "spiral" weaving of new and old and, at times, apparently divergent, learning together (p. 32-33).

My own understanding and experience of faith is also similar to that of Cornel West (2009). West proposes that just *being* is a form of risk, of faith (p. 9). He articulates how his faith philosophy and practice involve risking loving others, especially those whom society does not deem worthy of "love" and "wisdom" (p. 8-9). Through imagining possibilities where hope and purpose do exist even in the face of "the funk of life", in the midst of its materiality and dissonance, we create space for change (p. 23).

In faith, I have wrestled with a wide range of philosophical and practical issues, including: how and when to just *be*; how to honour and/or redeem what has already past with a reassurance of hope despite the likelihood of our failing again and again; and, how to delight in my embodied, relational, and spiritual insights and creativity so that I might employ them with "compassion" for myself and others (Nouwen 1990, p. 38-39; Palmer 2008, p. 5; Chodron 1994, p. xxviii, 5-6, 102). The character and dimension of my spiritual learning has immeasurably deepened due to the ongoing relationship and dialogue that I have had with my three spiritual directors during the last 17 years and the five church communities to which I have belonged. For their collective witness, example, and love I am incredibly grateful.

Writing as a Form of Creative Inquiry

Putting ink to page makes silence speak and the blank page signify.
(Dunlop 2007, p. 2-3)

It is my writing that has taught me how to pray and how to hope when I thought all hope was lost. In this process I practice the power of words and remind myself that each act is an intention, a prayer, and a re-envisioning of relationships. In contrast to first person narrative which chronicles one moment frozen in time and place and juxtaposes it with the next, poetry offers to me a metaphorical language to express deep spiritual and emotional learning; these poems use the power of metaphor to voice all that goes on inside us and yet is so rarely spoken aloud. Abandoning the detachment of analysis, poetry allows me to reveal my vulnerability and expose it further: through poetry I know more about myself with less certainty than ever before.

A Distracted Rendering

In awe of particular mysteries,
I reflect on ramblings of mind and pen
and discover myself
lost in a maze of presence.

Your voice seems
imperturbably silent,
the cacophony of living
and the din of doing
drown its tone
and muffle its timbre.

Your reflection appears opaque
and your face shrouded
sunk into the depths of
my image.

Stir my thoughts!
Shout your name!
Reveal yourself!

In the silence of the dark
I am wrapped in my soul's longings;
my pen speaks to the paper and
I am loved.

Contradiction in Mothering and Art

> The body now tak[en] on the shape of creation does not lessen my
> need for art. (Moraga 1997, p. 44)

Now that I have begun to identify myself as a creative person, I am able to understand why artists implore one another to "create for yourself and not care what anyone thinks" of your work, of your art (Penny 2008, p. 34). I am learning that creating, like mothering, requires a piece of me in each effort but that I must not take too much to heart what others think of my work since this can be far too costly to me and to my work.

However, I must confess that I care a great deal for what Bobby, in particular, thinks about my work, for indeed, he is a part of me. Like Clara, in *The Cruellest Month*, who "wanted the man who shared her soul to also share her vision", I want Bobby to embrace my vision (p. 35). Despite his initially telling me that he "did not get" my poetry when I began to write and share it with him, Bobby has done encouraged me in its pursuit and even more he has provided me with the support and the physical and mental space and time in which to do my writing (p. 34). Likewise, he has supported my passion for wrestling with my role and practice as a mother-educator and a teacher-leader (Wasley 1991). It took me many years to be certain that I am not being unfaithful to him, as a representative of the masculine, in critiquing male societal dominance, rather in pushing for mother learning possibilities for myself, I am creating new father learning opportunities for him, and new societal engagement opportunities for my daughters (Rich 1986, p. 283).

Words

I wait, waste not,
for words which
reach out
to your heart
and mind beneath.

Just as I long
to take back
that which I spoke before
in haste.

Those words
threatened to tear
the bonds we wove
in time,
with care
and grace.

Until *these* words,
a prayer inscribed:
I am,
I hope, and
I abide.

Prayer

During the last 10 years, at a distance from those for whom I care, I have felt increasingly disconnected from their lives and from invested relationships with them. When friends and family members are in crisis and I am unable to do what I know could be of practical assistance I often feel inadequate and find hope failing me. Prayer enables me to discern the presence of hope and how it binds us together. Such was the case when one of my nieces became very sick and I could not be with her or with the rest of my family. Writing of my anguish and of my love, framed by my faith and hope, became a source of encouragement to me and, I hope, to them.

For You

Though you are not my child
I imagine you as my own
when I gaze upon them resting peacefully in their beds.

I grieve for times and places
that I cannot be,
for those I cannot hold or hear,
for words and thoughts I cannot speak.

O little lamb, why you?
Why this? Why now?

There is so much we cannot understand
that makes us feel powerless
and enraged.
So we must trust,
and weep,
that the heaviness, which weighs upon our hearts might be lifted.

Your parents too are dear to me:
your mother's strength and joy,
your father's playfulness and open spirit,
their care for others,
their deep and passionate faith,

shine through your mischievous eyes and quick smile,
your sisters' big plans and imaginations.

I long for these:
for you,
for them,
and pray,
for this
I can do.

Hope

The concept of redemption is one that is often absent from our postmodern society, yet without it I could not make sense of the majority of my life. I had not acknowledged the wounding I had endured as a result of my miscarriage until I was in a context in which I was surrounded by others whose lives were defined by a desire to alleviate suffering and confess shame.

It was not until our church held a service to commemorate and dedicate the lives of children lost before or shortly after birth that I had even told Naia and Anica of my first pregnancy—a fact that also engendered shame in me. Rather than recognizing and naming my fragility in losing this child, even so many years later I succumbed to the expectation that it was yet another item that I had not achieved in my efforts to become the *perfect* parent.

Thankfully, many of my friends and community members who were present during the ceremony also had endured this grief, and our shared loss released me to celebrate the gift that this child could become for our family. The absence of pity or fear amongst those gathered blossomed into hope and mutual encouragement that remains with me still.

Cry for Joy

Trust,
never taught,
is layered and dismantled;
despite betrayal,
regardless of failure,
love silently triumphs over anguish.

In faith,

seemingly never strong enough,
lifted up;
pride masks truth,
fear and jealousy strangle love:
Yet love silently triumphs over anguish.

With
forgiveness,
redeemed and rediscovered;
from solitude,
broken
we gather.

Educational Principles & Practices

My writing enables me to discern the possibility for new life and new hope in the midst of limitations, loss, and disappointment. Through this outlet, I discovered that I wanted to affirm those who were seeking to parent wisely and thoughtfully.

Despite having gained more confidence in the value of my mothering and mother learning, I still felt I needed external validation of my knowledge and experience before I could become a parent educator. Thus I enrolled in the required certification program for US postnatal educators through the International Childbirth Education Association (ICEA). However, upon learning that *ICEA postnatal educators* are expected to be diagnosticians who must identify the problems of children and parents and utilize their expert knowledge to remedy them, I chose to complete the program with a different set of priorities in mind (2003, p. 3-13).

ICEA's mandate prioritizes the physical health a of each family member over everything else (2003, p. 9-12). Second, this institution expects its educators to focus on the "tasks" of parenting (p. 3; see also Ehrenreich & English 2005). This emphasis shifts all of the parents' attention to *what we must do for our children*, rather than reflecting upon and redefining *how we engage with* our children in complex and multi-dimensional relationships.

Conversely, as I nurtured my own children while studying in ICEA's postnatal education program, I realized that my goal was to become, and to support my child to become more than physically healthy. I also recognized that my role as an educator requires me to encourage, support, engage, and learn alongside other parent learners while providing them with knowledge of the wider resources available to them.

My desire to understand and resist traditional parenting discourses and experts, by discerning my own insights and expanding my network of support led me to apply to graduate school. Subsequently, Bobby and I returned to Vancouver with Naia after a year in Toronto and set about reconnecting with our church and our extended social communities in preparation for the birth of Anica and the beginning of my Masters of Education program at UBC. The experience of concurrently pursuing two contrasting educational programs has enriched my learning experience by teaching me to reflect upon the explicit principles and the implicit assumptions contained within personal, corporate, institutional systems and practices.

Educare - Lead

You tell me that *I* wouldn't have understood
even if you had told me,
but how do *you* know?

Make *no* assumptions,
ask *me* my thoughts,
inquire as to *my* experience and understanding.

If my ears aren't open
show me, so I can witness the truth.

Take me into *your* home
redefining goodness moment-by-moment,
in real time,
in story.

You
tell *me*
I'm a pessimist,
a complainer,
and a crazy person;
but *I* tell *you* the truth,
it's hard to be a mom
when you haven't had
an apprenticeship.

Let's abandon the silos
of our nuclear families.

Let the masters
speak up
and reach out
to the novices
so that the guild can be strengthened
in wisdom, perspective,
honesty, and experience
rather than numbers alone.

In intimacy *we* will be revealed.

Note: The following five narratives allude to some of the insights I gained through completing my practicum for ICEA's postnatal educator program. My practicum hours were divided between Women's Hospital and Health Centre's Reproductive Mental Health Program and Mamaspeak, an independent postnatal educator's private business.

April 14th Mamaspeak: On Format and Process

Immediately upon arriving at the first Mamaspeak session today, I noted that there were only women present. While that might seem obvious from the name of the organization, my first observation was to note the absence of fathers (since in this group all were heterosexual partnerships) in the group. As the discussion proceeded I was concerned at the amount of time the mothers spent criticizing their partners, and their fathering, without discussing how their partners might learn and be encouraged to be more positively engaged in parent learning.

However, once the women had the opportunity to articulate their frustrations, I was relieved to hear my practicum supervisor warn them that a great deal of damage could be done to both their spousal relationships and their child's relationship with their partner if they did not encourage their partner to actively participate in parent learning. Likewise, she highlighted that simply because their partners were not the primary caregiver that did not mean that they could not be a good parent or that being the primary caregiver meant that one was the sole authority on one's child's needs. At the same time, she impressed upon the mother learners that they must educate their partners about their own mother-needs since their spouses could not read their minds!

Therefore, while it is not ideal that fathers, in this case, or the breadwinners of any partnerships, are absent from a large part of the parent learning dialogue, it does not mean that they do not have experience or valuable insights to contribute. As I learned firsthand, if as mothers we are going to question our position as the default nurturer in the family, we have a responsibility to engage in dialogue with all of our children's alternate caregivers, and especially those who view themselves as the family breadwinners, in order to better clarify our specific family priorities and minimize the complications inherent in the parent learning process (Ross Epp & Cook 2004, p. 77, 88).[7]

Postscript:

Despite being skeptical about whether this particular class would stretch or challenge me as a parent educator, I quickly found myself drawn into the discussion about the challenges each mother mentioned facing at the time. My practicum supervisor's questions also prompted the mothers, of which there were 5 (1 of 6 being absent for the first two sessions), to reflect on the routines that they were beginning to structure for themselves and the expectations that were inherent within them. In addition, she inquired about their level of comfort or discomfort with the role in which they found themselves. Since only one of the moms expressed a sense of peace about her new role spoke at the end of the discussion, the other moms felt no qualms about articulating their struggles with adapting to the role of full-time caregiver and homemaker. In fact, the professionals, in particular, expressed having a more difficult time adjusting to the slower, yet no less demanding, pace of mothering.

While initially I found myself wondering why my practicum supervisor did not provide a more structured curriculum for the 2 groups she leads (one for moms of 0-6 month olds and the other for moms of 6-12 month olds) as I listened to the discussion, I soon recalled how little energy and concentration I had for books and other resources at that early stage of motherhood, and indeed how few I had found affirming. Afterwards I reflected on how my practicum supervisor's choice of Naomi Stadlen's (2004) book *What mothers do: especially when it looks like nothing* could hardly have been better affirmation for these women (p. 110-111). In doing so, she encouraged each woman to explore and learn at her own pace, while reminding them to try not being too critical of themselves. She challenged them to try to reduce their need for external validation by resisting the temptation to compare themselves to other mothers by locating themselves within the larger mothering story.

---

[7] I would also posit that this is an inherent weakness in the mother-blogging forums common on the internet (Gore 2000; Stadtman Tucker 2008).

Beyond the Near Enemy[8]

Like a filtering of star rays
memory of joyful intimacy

furrows the haze of yearning
bleeding into apathy

settling upon what lies
beneath our naked fear and needing

And on our beds
all our bitterness flown before the morning's light

we pause before all we've seen:
and reach for vulnerability.

April 19th Reproductive Mental Health: Is a Piece or All of Me Necessary to Mothering?

During one of my practicum sessions at Reproductive Mental Health's (RMH) Positive Parenting Program my postnatal education supervisor and I emphasized that mothers must challenge the judgments which are often deeply embedded in our evaluations of ourselves, our roles, and our abilities to fulfill the expectations of others through mothering our children (what my practicum supervisor referred to as our parenting beliefs (i.e. "I am a good mother/father when ...")

During this class I was struck by how regularly negative external messages can contribute to significant psychological, emotional, and even spiritual dysfunction/distress (especially when combined with biological factors, such as genetic predisposition). As the discussion progressed, I wondered whether or not I ought to disclose my own diagnosis of postpartum onset anxiety disorder so early in the program; I wondered whether sharing my experience of growth through this illness and the positive prognosis with which I now live would give others hope and deepen the level of intimacy and trust we shared or if instead it would compromise the fragile trust that we had only just begun to develop (Zingaro 2007). In this instance I discerned that I must get to know them better before divulging such intimate details since they would lack the context for my

---

[8] After reading Louise Penny's (2008) *The Cruellest Month*.

revelations (see **The Critic and Performer: A Letter to My Peers** for a more detailed discussion of this professional conflict).

Instead I chose to express how I often struggle with how much of myself I ought to be able to give to any one role in my life. Often I find myself doubting my ability to provide *enough* of what my kids need of my time, energy, and/or attention. In addition, I shared that I find myself just scraping by to satisfy the demands of my schoolwork and meager professional commitments while attending to my children's expectations of me.

Seemingly unanswerable questions arise on a regular basis. For example, do I spend too much of my already limited resources using the skills and talents which I have satisfying my daughters' desires by facilitating opportunities which will entertain and stimulate them or should I recognize my own boundaries and limitations and find them outside programs which will teach them skills and stretch them in ways which I cannot? If I choose the former am I adequately listening to, hearing, and attending to their needs that extend beyond our particular relationship or if I choose the latter am I just being a selfish and grumpy adult who values her own space above her relationship with her children (O'Brien Hallstein 2008; Hays 1996, p. 125-127)?

At times I see these struggles as costing me more than I can afford. On other occasions I am able to reach out to other caregivers, using additional resources and programs, to supplement my gifts so that I can encourage each child's unique development and creativity. These approaches are not dichotomous or exclusive of one another. Instead, I propose that my refined understanding of my role and identity as a caring and *good* mother includes sharing my gifts and resources among others in community rather than viewing my mentors, my peers, or my children as competing with me for what I have to offer.

It is easy to slip into an oppositional conception of parent and child in our self-focused society, but it is more challenging to attempt to discern how to consider each family member's needs simultaneously and to see one another as "gifts" to be cherished (Moraga 1997, p. 40). For the most part now, I am able to have the perspective to read the signs of both Naia's and Anica's behaviour and to understand the context for it, while also patiently helping them to understand *why* and *how* their behaviour must improve.

When I do react hastily and negatively to their demands because I have been making a conscious effort to give them a better quality, than quantity, of my presence, I am much more eager to apologize for any hurt I have caused, while clarifying my rationale for my behaviour, and diffusing the hostility between us. By challenging my assumptions and reflecting on the choices that I have made, I have learned to foster humility in myself while practicing one of the most encouraging aspects of communal parent learning.

Her-story: The Heart and Mind of a Woman

Unhinge me from my bit and bridle,
unsaddle me if you please.
The dustings and feedings,
tidy-ings and trappings,
give only temporary release.

In the belly or on the feet,
swallowed or trod beneath:
what is the place for pride,
the grief,
do I deserve to weep?

In the midst of numbers and signs,
I dissemble and, inevitably I keep
a feint of control, until I tremble--
and the ridiculous, I see.

What matters, has meaning
sustains and still seeming-ly
remains true and sure,
isn't built on effort,
achievement, nor beauty:
vanity, trust does not secure.

But its words that know, time to be,
that touch our empty souls.
So muddling through
and luminous, we
circle in twos and threes.

April 28th Mamaspeak: What's a Parent Worth These Days?

Whether it is reflected in the relationship between two spouses or trumpeted in the news, society's praise for certain parenting practices and/or opposition to others has a significant impact on how parents measure their self-worth and develop their self-confidence. Public esteem or scorn is a powerful tool in the motherhood discourse, in particular. At the same time the discrepancies between the monetary reward for the tasks and responsibilities of a breadwinner as opposed to a caregiver can undermine even the healthiest of partnerships and can cause them to doubt other aspects of their relationship.

These are only a few of the many ups and downs which parents have to face when learning about mothering and fathering. This has led me to reflect on what the role of parent education is in responding to the challenges with which parents wrestle on a daily basis. For example, parent educators can serve to oppose constraints imposed by cultural assumptions and uninformed external prejudices, thereby freeing learners to choose alternate ways of viewing their roles (Foucault 1984b p. 46-47). In order to do this effectively, they must possess a certain level of self-awareness in order to admit their challenges and doubts, while being open to the new mothering and fathering possibilities available to them.

Learners who find themselves constantly re-evaluating their role in the midst of being confounded by varied and astounding situations and interactions may regularly wonder at their how they will ever cope with being a parent (O'Brien Hallstein 2008, p. 107). Parent educators may facilitate connections between learners who share common doubts and questions despite having distinctly unique children and circumstances. Through humour that fosters humility, we may share our parenting foibles while celebrating our children's creativity and versatility. In this context, parent educators may provide learners with: support, perspective, and a context to affirm their own competency and resourcefulness; insight into their unmet parenting needs and desires; and, a new perspective that encourages them to view their children through more patient, compassionate, and loving eyes.

Finally, parent educators may give learners the opportunity to distill their priorities and clarify family guidelines that confirm their values by fostering ongoing flexibility through re-evaluation, dialogue, and compromise. Overall, affirming parent education does not seek to provide definitive solutions. Rather it *proposes* that parents seek to develop a philosophy and practices that are located somewhere between the seduction of complacency and a manic occupation with perfection.

May 5th Mamaspeak: Postpartum as Adjustment or Failure

Today my postnatal education supervisor opened the session by asking the mother learners to provide the group with a short summary of their general impressions of the post-partum period. The entire group concurred that they experienced the post-partum time as "overwhelming". Many members of the group described themselves as "going through the motions" during the first few weeks to two months, and being "anxious" to the point of being "compulsive" in their behaviours.

In addition, some of the mothers described themselves as experiencing a sense of loss as compared to the bond they felt had developed with the fetus during pregnancy; this was articulated by one mother in particular as feeling "empty" without the child inside of her. Conversely, one mother said she felt enormous relief at regaining some control of her body and no longer having what had felt like a "parasite" inside her.

The discussion transitioned from comments commonly shared among mothers who are seeking to prove their worth to one another to the more intimate experiences of mothers who have perceived themselves as failures as a result of having received a diagnosis of Post-Partum Depression (PPD). In her summary, my supervisor described this type of mental illness in a very astute way: as "a losing sight of the purpose and meaning in life". Two of the mothers in the group shared that they had received similar diagnoses, and one of them stated that she found herself "distraught" during the early transition to motherhood.

Cautioning the group against polarizing women's post-partum experiences by categorizing them as either positive or negative since neither extreme provides adequate depth of description, my supervisor introduced a quote from Lania Desmond, a counselor who emphasizes the identity shifts which occur for the woman during the pre-pregnancy, pre-natal, and post-partum periods "from wife to pregnant 'full' woman to mother". Desmond asserts that the change in the manner in which the mother cares for and communicates with her child is essentially wounding since, though while pregnant their relationship seems intuitive, it becomes more problematic when the child is outside of the woman's body and is unable to clearly communicate what it needs or wants (http://soulpoint.com/postpartum.html).

This description of the pregnancy and post-partum progression challenged each of us to re-envision the post-partum period. I wrestled with the inherently negative cast to Desmond's language, but found her acknowledgement of the challenges at the centre of the adjustment to parenting to be refreshing. Her naming this stage as a natural adaptation process, a journey that necessarily involves setbacks and learning and struggle proposes that mothering role has a very steep learning curve. Since our children provide us with very little coherent and consistent feedback (especially during the early stages) Desmond prompts us to view this period as an entirely new stage of life that is filled with opportunity for deepening the pivotal relationships in which we find ourselves, rather than seeking to return to a former understanding of normalcy.

Unable to present a perfect front of either being a perfect or entirely fulfilled mother I have fought against the idea that this results in my being an *impaired* mother. Though my own self-doubt and external criticism cause me to doubt my mother-value, the idea that I could, or I must, have perpetually positive emotions and perceptions has not resonated with me (Ehrenreich 2009). Instead I have determined that I must not let judgmental mother-critics have the last word on my mother-identity and mothering experience, instead I have sought to unearth what lies underneath and around my sentiments and rebuild my mother-self upon hope and compassion (Ladd-Taylor & Umansky 1998; Horowitz 2004; O'Reilly 2006; Gore 2000; Kinser 2008).

In response to the discussion about Desmond's interpretation of the transition to mothering I spoke up in an effort to affirm the resourcefulness of each of the mothers present in seeking out additional support. I went on to encourage them for their evident openness to possibility, growth, and change by being present in a context for learning and personal growth.

Redemption in Possibility[9]

Blossom scorched and drowned exceeds calculation
yet frailty dares to stretch and strain
to seek freedom where lacks momentum
until surprised by gleam and flutter
revealing breath and imagination
may Pandora retain her grasp
on the gem in her possession
restoring to us in the moment
the sums of grace ad infinitum

May 12th Mamaspeak: 'Birthstories', Impressions Not Pronouncements

Having designed her program with the goal of respecting confidences and gradually building trust, my postnatal education supervisor chose to reserve the sharing of birth stories until the final class in the series of six. In doing so, she relayed to us that she hoped we would be able to present our *impressions* of the experience (i.e. the primary challenges and pre-eminent joys) rather than simply a timeline of events, as is usually encouraged by those who request to hear a mother's birth story after the fact.

Listening to each of the six women speak of their experiences I was astounded by the wide range of painful experiences that these women recounted. In addition, each person's reflections confirmed the value of trusting one's instincts as a mother in the face of either opposition or contradictions. Even those women who honoured their gut feelings, did not exempt themselves from self-recrimination for confirmation of their instincts, but shouldered a great deal of anxiety about what could have happened had they not stood firm. Many of the mothers articulated their personal hurt and disappointment in the form of unmet or unresolved expectations they had of themselves, others, and of the event itself. They included the following examples ...

Area of Concern for mother	Expectation was that ____ would be able to:	Experience was that ____ was:
Spouse/Partner	• provide unique and intimate support	• absent, • emotionally distant, and/or • less than capable

---

[9] After reading Louise Penny's (2008) *The Murder Stone*.

103

Area of Concern for mother	Expectation was that _____ would be able to:	Experience was that _____ was:
Maternal Grandmother	• listen to and respect the couple's decisions and desires	• judgmental, • controlling, and/or • emotionally distant
Professionals/ Caregivers/ Medical System	• be professional, • be efficient, • be decisive, and • be caring beyond reproach	• overworked, • businesslike yet distant, • neglectful, and/or • disrespectful to the mother and/or her family
Self	• handle the pain, • be flexible, and • modify own expectations in the moment, as need demands	• desperate for medication, and yet/or • wrestling with the loss of control
Birth	• go smoothly, and • lack complications	• slow and draining, or • an emergency situation

In particular, one of the most striking realizations for me was the depth of wounding which can occur as a result of the words and actions of others during such a defined, yet formative period in time. We, mothers, subject ourselves, and are subjected, to incredible quantities of criticism for our role, our values, and our practices. All of these comments confirmed for me that physical healing occurs at light speed when compared with emotional and psychological healing.

Resistance

"Quiet desperation"[10]
no more,
only courage
to speak out

of the loneliness
that eats away

of the hope
that is lost

---

[10] Frank and April Wheeler, from Richard Yates' *Revolutionary Road*, discuss that even if it makes them insane to resist the status quo, they will persist with their resistance. Unfortunately, Frank concedes defeat by giving in to society's expectations of success for a young man in the business world leaving April concluding despairingly that she must indeed be insane for continuing to want to resist such expectations.

of the expectations
that are dashed

of the betrayal
that cuts so deep

of the drudgery
that breaks down

of the self
that disappears ....

unless we trust our insights,
risk ridicule and exclusion,
resist the anonymity, and
recommit every moment to the truth
we will not live to love
but in spite of it.

The Study of Motherhood While Mothering

I am not dissatisfied with either of my roles, of student/writer or of mother, but am torn by the conflict between the two. For as Chandler (1998) writes, being both "is an existence fraught with tension, for while each site demands my attention, the former requires quiet sustained concentration, [and] the latter the alertness of a catcher behind home plate, neither allow[ing] me to inhabit the other adequately" (p. 271). Pulled in these two disparate directions at times stretches me so thin, I fear I might break.

Mother learning is all about *being depended on*, while seeking out those whom *we can be dependent upon* to support us and care for our children alongside of us (Chandler 1998, p. 284). Mothering is not about asserting one's independence through expending all of one's energy to fight against our dependence on others and their dependence upon us. By modeling loving interdependence upon one another within a nuclear family, an extended family, friendships, mentorships, workplaces, schools, churches (or other religious groups), and other communities, we are teaching our children about our inextricable ties to those with whom we live and learn.

Mother Leader

The Critic and the Performer: A Letter to My Peers

The temptation for me is to wish that I can create a clear and simple product, a mothering how-to guide that could instruct mothers on how to practice only fulfilling and loving parenting. There is no definitive list of such practices.

However, even if that were possible, I would be required to be open about my struggles as a mother, exposing both the systemic constraints on my mothering and my many errors in judgment. I am never certain to what extent I ought to do this. As an educator, how do I honour my doubts as well as my need to have others accept me despite my shortcomings (Ladd-Taylor & Umansky 1998, p. 133, 139)? I am still seeking more ways to honestly build bridges and inspire respect and trust in other parent learners.

The more that I gain confidence as a parent educator, the more I realize that as both a practitioner and an educator, as a mother and a guide for other parents, as a "bordered professional", I must delineate which communities I define as personal and in which I will choose to identify myself a leader (Zingaro 2007). I walk a very fine line between revealing too much of myself, and divulging too little of the insight I have gained through experience and discernment. Therefore, through the disclosure carefully considered personal revelations I seek to create a pathway into the parent learning dialogue and encourage others to trust me and my insights enough to risk engaging in our conversation.

For example, through this collection of writing I have articulated in much detail how my own doubts and challenges have influenced my teaching, my motivations, and my goals. However, when teaching I would not reveal as much detail since it might cause participating parent learners to fear that they too must reveal so much, even too much, detail if they want to engage in the learning process (Taylor & Jarecke 2009, p. 279). My challenge both as a mother and as an educator will be to view the daily unknowns of mothering and teaching not as an overwhelming burden, but rather as opportunities which challenge me to model taking considered risks, while being artful and innovative (Taylor & Jarecke 2009, p. 287. One way that I can do this in the context of learning is to model and foster a "playful" environment characterized by welcome, grace, and humour, which Davis, Sumara, and Luce-Kapler (2000) stress can provide illumination through "surprising insights" (p. 148).

This understanding has enabled me to discern when and how much of myself as mother-learner and mother-educator to reveal in order to enrich the mother learning dialogue and not stifle it. Through this process I am seeking to create "a family of women" and men that may draw mother and father learners beyond the "motherhood" ideal and into a view of "empowered mothering" and fathering (Moraga 1997, p.54; O'Reilly 2006, p. 16; Horowitz 2004, p. 54-55). It is my hope that " by exploring mothering and learning through lived inquiry and practice rich with imaginative possibilities each learner can move beyond detached critical analysis to an embodied, relational, and spiritual knowing that is intimate, incisive, and inclusive.

The Teacher Parent

Awoken by clocks, groans, and sighs,
girding for battle, or lulled by cries,
muddling or revving towards the daily fray,
is clocking in at the breakfast cafe.

Sorting lunches, notes and gear,
planning, prepping, and lending an ear,
herding bodies out into the dawning gray,
for studies, practice, creation, and play.

For despite her papers, know-how, and training,
her insight's still weak and often waning,
preoccupied with details and quick to display
her short fuse, frustration, and general dismay.

Yet,
away from hers and listening to you,
she learns to risk, and trust anew,
to reflect on parents as "jars of clay"[11],
hoping their faith and love they convey.

---

[11] From 2 Corinthians Chapter 4, verse 7.

How to Lead?

In a mothers' group that I have been leading recently, the volatile group dynamics have hindered my ability to lead the group in reflective learning. There have been two barriers to my expressing and following through on my teaching priorities in this group. First, some of the mothers in this group have had long standing conflicts that they regularly revisit. This in turn, draws the leaders and the remaining group members into the dispute and halts the learning process.

In order to protect the group relationships and dissipate the tension I proposed a two-pronged approach using Freire's "problem-posing" technique (Taylor & Jarecki 2009, p. 284-285). Through private discussion between the leaders and the women involved in the conflict I suggested that together we could examine the source of their conflict and how it was influencing, perhaps even damaging, the health of the community. Secondly, I advised that we participate in careful and intentional group dialogue about what the group's behavioural guidelines needed to be and how we could work together to maintain them (Taylor & Jarecki 2009, p. 278).

While my co-leaders initially agreed to my proposal, one in particular did not adopt this approach wholeheartedly but granted each individual increasingly more time to consider their personal perspective. In the interim the group was not able to proceed with deeper learning but stalled due to the absence of mutual trust. After one volatile small group meeting my colleague articulated two concerns: first, she clarified that she was uncomfortable with confrontation and would prefer not to speak with the individuals concerned regarding the specifics of the conflict; and, second, she felt it was inappropriate for the group to discuss how individual conflicts interfered with group dynamics, even in general terms, since the group members might unjustly judge the specific women affected by this particular conflict.

However, after allowing the negativity to fester for almost a month and a half from when the conflict had first arisen I could definitely observe that the level of discomfort in the group was continuing to rise to the point where previously consistent attendees were regularly absent and others were uncomfortable engaging in the most innocuous group discussions. Increasingly I felt inhibited by the hands-off approach my colleague was promoting and knew that I was being forced to behave in a manner in direct conflict with my training as both a group counselor and as an educator. Despite my reluctance to contradict her, I was spurred to speak out against what was threatening isolation and the disintegration of trust in our community.

When I finally realized that my co-leader would not seize any of the multiple opportunities to foster dialogue and when some members of the community began expressing their feelings of exclusion from the group as a whole, I realized that the situation was in immediate danger of jeopardizing the safety of the community over the long term. Convinced that decisive action was necessary, with the support of another colleague, I took ownership for the lack of leadership provided in this matter.

In conversation with the women involved in this conflict alone, we discussed the particulars of their conflict and acknowledged that in some cases people involved in a disagreement must be willing to agree to disagree, yet live in harmony. Finally, together we clarified how they might each take responsibility for how this disagreement was negatively influencing the whole group. Afterwards we came together with the group as a whole and elicited from everyone what their priorities were for group communication and interaction (Taylor & Jarecki 2009, p. 287). Despite my fears that certain members of the group had radically retreated, when a new crisis for one group member arose, it was clear that sufficient trust had been restored to the group when that member reached out to the others for support and they responded with welcome, affirmation, and caring.

Since that time, the group has invested a lot of their energies in investigating how negative interactions have limited their ability to learn from the experiences, questions, doubts, and gathered wisdom of others, particularly in their families. At the same time, many of the members have articulated how they have come to see conflict as an opportunity for learning and growth, both individually and communally (Dickau 2010b; Hof 2010).

Compromise

When at first I heard those words
the shock was all I felt,
but soon the anger overtook
and led me where I went.

Ranting to another [I ceased for a time],
gripped by resolve, and your inertia,
I acted upon what conviction told me I should.
Still in my being, I held resentment
and questioned your ability to lead.

With your apology, I acquiesced,
a sigh heard escaping my lips.
Later, exhausted, I revisited the path
down which I had fled,
but beyond the moment I found disappointment
and, not strangely, fear had stayed my hand.

A week in limbo I wondered what future
there was in this for us.
Yet right from the door
your hand guided everything,
dipping in carefully,
you faced each of us.

Honestly, I knew you two years ago
for even a lifetime won't erase
the moment I saw our reflections:
me needing you, needing me,
leading us to where we find ourselves.

The Origins of Dialogue in Adult Education

> Freire's dialogic learning "gave students dignity. It placed the teacher at
> their side, with the task of orienting and directing the educational process
> but ... also in the act of searching ... also a learner. (Gadotti 2006, p. 2)

Paulo Freires theory and practice deeply inspired me during my first course of
graduate school. His desire to empower and equip marginalized workers with critical
thinking skills while fostering creative growth in their learning process, spurred me to
abandon the assumption that critical thinking skills are the knowledge capital of the
privileged classes (Freire 2000, p. 81; 84). His emphasis on communal inquiry, that saw
both educators and learners as "*becoming*--as unfinished, uncompleted beings in and
with a likewise unfinished reality"—who are seeking both knowledge and ultimately
mutual growth through relationship, challenges me to remain humble, while honouring
the learners' needs for respect and safety (italics in original, p. 84; 80-81). This truth has
been further revealed to me by the wise and resourceful single mothers whom I now

serve; in their experience of capriciousness and their hope for grace these mothers daily teach me about the costs of both complacency and despair, the role of resistance, and the centrality of faith.

> The pursuit of full humanity, however, cannot be carried out in isolation or individualism, but only in fellowship and solidarity. (Freire 2000, p. 85)

Learning and Listening: Dialogue in Practice

Educators Anthony Clarke and Steve Collins (2007) emphasize the value of an educator who will engage learners in a more meaningful way by moderating, their own, "purposeful discourse" (p. 167). I start all group discussions by inviting parents to express the constraints that hinder their parent learning in particular contexts. Once they articulate their frustrations with and anxieties about externally imposed or internally adopted parenting ideals, I provide them with the opportunity to reflect upon and discuss how they might want to redefine their parent learning priorities and practices. Providing them with time and space in which to critique discourses and the impact that these have upon their family lives is liberating for them. I follow this discussion with examples of the hope offered by considering alternate parenting possibilities.

I provide no specific lesson plans, but propose that educators prepare insightful, encouraging, and creative resources for parent learners and be willing to abandon their agenda if and when the need arises. Learners' specific needs can rarely be anticipated. Educators must remain flexible and open to learning opportunities as they present themselves, responding to learners' desires to explore new challenges.

However, as linear as this process appears, it is not since, often, the parent learners are considering multiple scenarios and dynamics at the same time as one another. First, we must recognize the limitations that we each possess in understanding our own, let alone one another's, learning goals and priorities. Second, we must seek to understand the fluid nature of all learning as cyclical, contemplative, imaginative, and active before we can engage in sharing knowledge and seeking to transform ourselves and our practices (Nelson 2000, pp. 259, 263; Merton 1972, p. 273; Sinner, et al. 2006). Only when we recognize that learning is an ongoing process that is evolving and changing throughout our living, can we embrace the complexity of engaging in learning together and seek to learn dynamically and openly.

Parent learners must develop a new understanding of themselves as *a learner*, one who is "becoming" and who is *on "the road"*, rather than one who must reach the destination of perfect insight and complete knowledge (Taylor & Jarecki 2009, p. 281; Luther 1521; Nelson 2000, p. 268; Shaia & Gaugi 2010, p. 243). Only then my they begin to *learn how to be* in the company of their child(ren) and their fellow learners.

"This life, therefore

is not righteous
but growth in righteousness

not health but healing
not being but becoming
not rest but exercise.

We are not yet what we shall be
but we are growing toward it,
the process is not yet finished
but it is going on,
this is not the end
but it is the road.

All does not yet gleam in glory
but all is being purified."

Martin Luther (1521) *Defense of All the Articles*

When possible, I suggest that learners employ alternate methods of inquiry and self-examination to push beyond the limits of conventional, rational reflection and analysis (Taylor & Jarecki 2009, p. 286). I invite learners to engage in discussion with their partners, alternate caregivers, and child(ren) in an effort to articulate and foster their family values and priorities. In the second phase of this activity, I suggest that they do a reflective writing or artistic exercise that depicts how they discerned a particular value was a priority for their family. Finally, I suggest that the individual learners use another method to evaluate how well their families commit to and affirm these priorities. Learners can use these creative methods to identify which family concerns are priorities which they want to address and resolve. In addition, they can use these methods to invest and engage in a more profound understanding of the complexities of parent knowing and decision-making, thereby getting a richer and more varied learning experience in the process.

In order to maximize the group's learning and invite a greater level of trust and intimacy, I conclude the activity by moderating a discussion during which each learner is welcome to share personal insights and concerns. This practice encourages learners to model humility and seek accountability. In being attuned to each learner through In being attuned to each learner, through "listening" to their words and "scrutinizing" their behaviour, I may discern when to prompt them, when to encourage them, and when to challenge them (Karpiak 2000a, pp. 38-39). I must remain alert, stepping in to stimulate discussion that is lagging, or weaving in gems that may unsettle complacent learners, in order to nurture more "fruitful" results, illustrate how each learner is realizing their learning, and "celebrate" the advent of their learning (Clarke & Collins 2007, p. 167; Taylor & Jarecki 2009, p. 278; Nelson 2000, p. 268).

However, by employing Freire's problem-posing process I may push the learners "beyond the rational" into embodied, emotional, and spiritual reflection, drawing out deeply felt experiences (Taylor & Jarecki 2009, p. 280, 282, 284). As a result of this vulnerability, I must be vigilant in preserving a respectful and forgiving environment that waits upon each learner's story and acknowledges the tension between, fear of failure and judgment and, the need for grace and compassion (Nouwen 1990, p. 94; Palmer 2008, p. 5; Taylor & Jarecki 2009, p. 282). By using compassion in an effort to gain mutual understanding we may attempt to take risks within the group learning process that promote intimacy and self-awareness (Brach 2003, p. 313, 295; Nouwen 1990, p. 88-89).

This invitation invites learners to consider which ideas take prominence, which are developed, and which are resolved or dismissed, depending on the level of importance to them personally. In turn, if the learner wishes to work on an activity on their own time, they can limit how many people see and hear their thoughts thereby controlling the level of personal risk in which they are engaging. Finally, learners can use alternate learning models to invest in deeper learning, thereby getting a richer and more varied learning experience in the process.

This multilayered learning process that encourages a variety of approaches to adult learning may provide a more profound understanding of the complexities of parent knowledge and decision-making. At the same time it prompts individual learners to practice both "reflexivity and transparency" which fosters accountability and welcomes engagement with "the unexpected, the unusual, and the unanticipated" (Smith 2000, p. 143; Clarke & Collins 2007, p. 167, 169).

Change

Blundering interruptions
a nuisance?
Reflected whispers
jog our memory.

Vast, cold, deep ...
with change is suddenly
delightful and comforting.

Child-like radiance
playfully dancing,
sparkling across the rippling mirror.

Listening leads to gratitude;
filled with grace,
respond with thanksgiving
and herald conversation of a new variety.

Friendship redefined.
Unexpected, blessed
beauty.

Conclusion

The learning that new mothers undertake is substantial, yet it has not received widespread attention in adult education literature. Through preparing for and writing my thesis I have sought to chronicle my journey from novice mother to mother learner and parent educator by employing the same "reflexivity and transparency" that I challenge others to employ (Smith 2000, p. 141, 143, 149).

Before guiding parents through their learning process I first had to understand my own. Naming and critiquing the diverse and variable dimensions which have been inherent in my own mother-learning process has enabled me to claim those discourses that have built in me a resolve to resist and question subjugating discourses while claiming my own mother learning process and the knowledge and meanings inherent within it. My autobiographical writing, my analytical research, and my parent education philosophy, has enabled me to confess my biases and describe my context while illustrating my processes of discernment, fostering creative learning, and engaging others in a dynamic parent learning dialogue. Mother-learners and educators, myself included, can modify, re-enact and integrate our learning into the collective mother knowledge through a combination of discernment, exploration, planning, action, and experimentation (Kolb 1984; Hill 2008; Freiler 2008; Beckett 1998, as referenced in Fenwick 2001, p. 246).

By reflecting upon how the context, experience, and conclusions of each mother and father learner that I have encountered were similar or different than my own I have claimed the mother knowing and knowledge which defines me (Piantanida, Garman & McMahon 2000, p. 99-100; Springgay, Irwin & Wilson Kind 2005, p. 899). In order to validate the unique insights and lived experience of my fellow mother and father learners I sought to gain insight into their shared and distinct identities and work (Willis 2000, p. 37). Through my autobiographical writings, my analytical research, and my teaching I have begun to discern new means of learning, being, and mothering. These creative processes of inquiry can assist in refining existing pedagogical approaches to parent education, and can foster new ones that embody the tension and the depth inherent in the parent learning process.

My mother writing, research and teaching have been rich in wisdom, grace and joy revealed in bodily, relational, and spiritual insights. Through them I have also redeemed the label of *stay-at-home mom*. In hindsight I can see this role as more than a sole-identifier of my person, rather as a descriptor of the location and the relationships that I deem to be my primary focus. By claiming this role I have moved from a state of constant "ambivalence" to one of declaration (Tuley 2008: 163; Stadlen 2004: 151).

Declaration

I am a vital and creative woman,
an articulate and resourceful mother, and
a strong and nurturing leader
illuminating the dark corners of power and poverty,
and effecting change.

References

International Childbirth Education Association (ICEA). (2003). Postpartum as a process and the role of the postnatal educator. In L. Todd (Ed.), *ICEA postnatal educator certification program: Study Modules* (Study Module I, pp. 3-13). Minneapolis, MN: ICEA.

ICEA. (2003). Position statement and review of postpartum emotional disorders. In L. Todd (Ed.), *ICEA postnatal educator certification program: Study Modules* (III, pp. 1-7). Minneapolis, MN: ICEA.

Pacific Postpartum Support Society (2002). *Postpartum depression and anxiety* (6th ed.). Vancouver, BC: Pacific Postpartum Support Society.

Aragon, J. (2008). Instinctual Mamahood: How I found the mama. In J. Nathanson & L. C. Tuley (Eds.) *Mother knows best: Talking back to the "experts"* (pp. 167-173). Toronto, ON: Demeter Press.

Aron, E. A. (2002). *The highly sensitive child: Helping our children thrive when the world overwhelms them.* New York, NY: Broadway Books.

Aston, M. L. (2002). Learning to be a normal mother: Empowerment and pedagogy in postpartum classes. *Public Health Nursing, 19* (4), 284-293.

Ball, A. (2006). Everyone's Waiting [Television Series Episode]. In *Six feet under.* New York, NY: Home Box Office (HBO).

Barndt, D. (2001). Naming, making, connecting—reclaiming the lost arts: The pedagogical possibilities of photo-story production In Pat Campbell & Barbara Burnaby (Eds.), *Participatory Practices in Adult Education* (pp. 31- 54). London: Lawrence Erlbaum Associates.

Bobel, C. (2008). Resisting, but not too much: Interrogating the paradox of natural mothering. In J. Nathanson & L. C. Tuley (Eds.) *Mother knows best: Talking back to the "experts"* (pp. 113-123). Toronto, ON: Demeter Press.

Boreen, J. & Niday, D. (2000). Breaking through the isolation: Mentoring beginning teachers. *Journal of Adolescent and Adult Literacy, 44* (2), 152-164.

Bourdieu, P. & Passeron, J.-C. (1977 [1970]). *Reproduction in education, society, culture.* (R. Nice, Trans.). London: Sage Publications.

Brach, T. (2003). *Radical acceptance: Embracing your life with the heart of a Buddha.* New York, NY: Bantam Books.

Burrell, G. (1988). Modernism, Post Modernism and Organizational Analysis 2: The Contribution of Michel Foucault. *Organization Studies*, 9 (2), 221-235.

Butler, J. (2004). On the limits of sexual autonomy. In *Undoing gender* (pp. 17-39). New York, NY: Routledge.

Butler S. & Bentley, R. (1996). *Lifewriting: Learning through personal narrative.* Scarborough, ON: Pippin Publishing.

Butt, R. & Raymond, D. (1989). Studying the nature and development of teachers' knowledge using collaborative autobiography. *International Journal of Educational Research* 13 (4), 403-419.

Byrne-Armstrong, H. (2001). Re-authoring self: Knowing as being. In H. Byrne-Armstrong, J. Higgs & D. Horsfall (Eds.), *Critical moments in qualitative research* (pp. 68-78). Oxford: Butterworth-Heinemann.

Capra, F. (1994). *Ecology and community.* (pp. 1-10). Berkeley, CA: Centre for Ecoliteracy. Retrieved April 12, 2009 from www.ecoliteracy.org/index.html

Chandler, M. (1998). Emancipated subjectivities and the subjugation of mothering practices. In S. Abbey & A. O'Reilly (Eds.), *Redefining motherhood: Changing identities and patterns* (pp. 270-286). Toronto, ON: Second Story Press.

Clandinin, D. J. & Rosiek, J. (2007). Mapping a landscape of narrative inquiry: Borderland spaces and tensions. In D. J. Clandinin (Ed.), *Handbook of narrative inquiry: Mapping a methodology* (pp. 35-75). Thousand Oaks, CA: Sage Publications, Inc.

Clarke, A. & Collins, S. (2007). Complexity science and student teacher supervision. In *Teaching and Teacher Education,* 23, 160-172.

Code, L. (1991). *What can she know? Feminist theory and the construction of knowledge.* Ithaca, NY: Cornell University Press.

Daly, K. (2004). The changing culture of parenting. *Contemporary Family Trends series.* Ottawa, ON: The Vanier Institute of the Family. Unpaginated. Retrieved May 3, 2008 from http://www.vifamily.ca/library/cft/parenting.html

Davis, B. & Sumara, D. (1998). Unskinning curriculum. In W.F. Pinar (Ed.), *Curriculum: Toward New Identities* (pp. 75-92). New York, NY: Garland Publishing Inc.

Davis, B., Sumara, D. & Luce-Kapler, R. (2000). *Engaging minds: Learning and teaching in a complex world.* Mahwah, NJ: Lawrence Erlbaum Associates, Publishers.

Dewey, J. (1934). *Art as experience*. New York, NY: The Berkeley Publishing Group.

Dickau, T. (2010a). *Facing life's pressures: Hebrews 4:14-16; 7:24-28; 8:6-13.* Presented on May 2nd to the congregations of Grandview Calvary Baptist Church.

Dickau, T. (2010b). *"He loved me and gave himself for me": Luke 22:63-23:26.* Presented on March 21st to the congregations of Grandview Calvary Baptist Church.

Dobson, J. (1983). *The strong-willed child: Birth through adolescence (12th ed.).* Wheaton, IL: Tyndale House Publishers, Inc.

Dreikurs, R. & Stolz, V. (1964). *Children: The challenge*. New York, NY: Plume.

Dunlop, R. (1998). Written on the Body. In S. Abbey & A. O'Reilly (Eds.), *Redefining motherhood: Changing identities and patterns* (pp. 103-124). Toronto, ON: Second Story Press.

Dunlop, R. (Ed.) (2007). *White Ink: Poems on mothers and motherhood*. Toronto, ON: Demeter Press.

Eakin, P. J. (1999). *How our lives become stories*. Ithaca, NY: Cornell University Press.

Ehrenreich, B (2009). Bright-sided: *How the relentless promotion of positive thinking has undermined America*. New York, NY: Metropolitan Books.

Ehrenreich, B & English, D. (2005). *For her own good: Two centuries of the experts' advice to women* (2nd ed.). New York, NY: Anchor Books.

Faber, A. & Mazlish, E. (1999). *How to talk so kids will listen & listen so kids will talk (2nd ed.).* New York, NY: HarperCollins Publishers, Inc.

Fairclough, N. (1992). *Discourse and social change*. Cambridge: Polity Press.

Featherstone, B. (2003). Taking Fathers Seriously. *British Journal of Social Work*, 33, 239-254.

Fenwick, T. (2001). Work knowing 'On the Fly': Enterprise cultures and co-emergent epistemology. *Studies in Continuing Education* 23 (2), 243-259.

Fenwick, T. (2003a). *Learning through experience: Troubling orthodoxies and intersecting questions*. Malabar, FL: Krieger Publishing Company.

Fenwick, T. (2003b). Reclaiming and re-embodying experiential learning through complexity science. *Studies in the Education of Adults*, 35 (2), 123-141.

Foley, G. (1999). *Learning in social action: A contribution to understanding informal education.* New York, NY: Zed Books.

Foucault, M. (1984a). What is critique? In L. Hochroth & S. Lotringer (Eds.), *The politics of truth* (pp. 23-82). New York, NY: Semiotext(e).

Foucault, M. (1984b). What is enlightenment? In P. Rabinow (Ed.), *The Foucault Reader* (pp. 32-50). New York, NY: Pantheon.

Freeman, M. (2007). Autobiographical understanding and narrative inquiry. In D. J. Clandinin (Ed.), *Handbook of narrative inquiry: Mapping a methodology* (pp. 120-145). Thousand Oaks, CA: Sage Publications, Inc.

Freiler, T. (2008). Learning through the body. *New Directions for Adult and Continuing Education,* 119 (Fall), 37-47.

Freire, P. (2000). *Pedagogy of the oppressed* (30th anniversary ed.) (M. Bergman Ramos, Trans.). New York, NY: Continuum.

Geertz, C. (2003). Thick description: Toward an interpretive theory of culture. In N. K. Denzin & Y. S. Lincoln (Eds.), *Turning points in qualitative research: Tying knots in a handkerchief* (pp. 143-168). Walnut Creek, CA: AltaMira Press.

Gaodotti, M. (2005). Paulo Freire: A homage, on http://www.nl.edu/academics/cas/ace/resources/Documents/FreireHomage.cfm downloaded on March 22, 2010.

Green, F. (2004). Feminist mothers: Successfully negotiating the tensions between motherhood as 'institution' and 'experience'. In A. O'Reilly (Ed.), *Mother outlaws: Theories and practices of empowered mothering,* (pp. 31-42). Toronto, ON: Women's Press.

Green, F. (2008). Feminist motherline: Embodied knowledge/s of feminist mothering. In A. O'Reilly (Ed.), *Feminist Mothering,* (pp. 161-176). New York, NY: State of New York Press.

Grumet, M. (1987). The politics of personal knowledge. *Curriculum Inquiry* 17 (3), 319-329.

Grumet, M. (1988). *Bitter milk: Women and teaching.* Amherst, MA: The University of Massachusetts Press.

Hall, N. (1980). *The moon and the virgin: Reflections on the archetypal feminine.* New York, NY: HarperTrade.

Hansman, C. A. (2001). Context-based adult learning. *New Directions for Adult and Continuing Education*, 89, 43-52.

Hart, M. U. (1992). *Working and educating for life: feminist and international perspectives on adult education*. New York, NY: Routledge.

Hartnett, S. J. & Engels, J. D. (2008). "Aria in a time of war": Investigative poetry and the politics of witnessing. In N. K. Denzin & Y. S. Lincoln (Eds.), *Collecting and interpreting qualitative materials* (3rd ed.) (pp. 587-622). Thousand Oaks, CA: Sage Publications, Inc.

Hays, S. (1996). *The cultural contradictions of motherhood*. New Haven, CN: Yale University Press.

Helfenbaum, W. (2009). My dirty little secret--I was a breastfeeding bust. *BC Parent* Fall, 8-9.

Hewett, H. (2008). Of motherhood born. In A. E. Kinser (Ed.), *Mothering in the Third Wave* (pp. 19-30). Toronto, ON: Demeter Press.

Hill, R. J. (2008). Troubling Adult Learning in the Present Time. *New Directions for Adult and Continuing Education*, 119 (Fall), 83-92.

Hill Collins, P. (1994). Shifting the center: Race, class, and feminist theorizing about motherhood. In D. Bassin, M. Honey & M. M. Kaplan (eds.), *Representations of motherhood* (pp. 56-74). New Haven, CT & London: Yale University Press.

Hof, M. (2010). *Responding to the cross: Luke 23:26-49*. Presented on March 28th to the congregations at Grandview Calvary Baptist Church.

Holman-Jones, S. (2003). The way we were, are, and might be: Torch singing as autoethnography. In N. K. Denzin & Y. S. Lincoln (Eds.), *Turning points in qualitative research: Tying knots in a handkerchief* (pp. 105-118). Walnut Creek, CA: AltaMira Press.

Holman-Jones, S. (2008). Autoethnography: Making the personal political. In N. K. Denzin & Y. S. Lincoln (Eds.), *Collecting and interpreting qualitative materials* (3rd ed.) (pp. 205-246). Thousand Oaks, CA: Sage Publications, Inc.

hooks, b. (1990). Homeplace: A Site of Resistance. In *Yearning: Race, gender, and cultural politics* (pp. 41-49). Boston, MA: South End Press.

Horowitz, E. (2004). Resistance as a site of empowerment: The journey away from maternal sacrifice. In A. O'Reilly (Ed.), *Mother Outlaws: Theories and Practices of Empowered Mothering* (pp. 43-57). Toronto, ON: Women's Press.

Horowitz, E. & B. C. Long, (2005). Mothering and stress discourses: A deconstruction of the interrelationship of discourses on mothering and stress. In M. Porter, P. Short & A. O'Reilly (Eds.), *Motherhood: Power and oppression* (pp. 97-110). Toronto, ON: Women's Press.

Howard, C. (ed.) (2007). *Between interruptions: 30 women tell the truth about motherhood.* Toronto, ON: Key Porter Books Limited.

Iovine, V. (1997). *The girlfriend's guide to surviving the first year of motherhood.* New York, NY: Perigree.

Irwin, R. L. (2004). A/r/tography: A metonymic metissage. In R. L. Irwin & A. de Cosson (Eds.), *a/r/tography: Rendering Self Through Arts-based Living Inquiry* (pp. 27-38). Vancouver, BC: Pacific Educational Press.

Jagger, A. M. (1989). Love and knowledge: Emotion in feminist epistemology. *Inquiry,* 32 (2), 151-176.

Johnson B. & Solem, J. (Eds.) (2007). *Respectful responsible parenting: A facilitator's guide* (Revised Ed.). Saskatoon, SK: Saskatoon Adlerian Society.

Karpiak, I. (2000a). Evolutionary theory and the 'new sciences': Rekindling our imagination for transformation. *Studies in Continuing Education,* 22 (1), 29-44.

Karpiak, I. (2000b). Writing our life: Adult learning and teaching through autobiography. *Canadian Journal of University Continuing Education* 26 (1), 31-50.

Karpiak, I. (2005). More than artistry: The integral aspect of autobiography. *Canadian Journal of University Continuing Education* 31 (1), 87-107.

Kenyon G. M. & Randall, W. L. (1997). *Restorying our lives: Personal growth through autobiographical reflection.* Westport, CT: Praeger.

Kincheloe, J. L. & Berry, K. S. (2004). *Rigour and complexity in educational research: Conceptualizing the bricolage.* New York, NY: Open University Press.

Kinser, A. E. (2008a). Introduction. In A. Kinser (Ed.) *Mothering in the Third Wave* (pp. 1-16). Toronto, ON: Demeter Press.

Kinser, A. E. (2008b). Mothering as relational consciousness. In A. OReilly (Ed.) *Feminist Mothering* (pp. 123-140). Albany, NY: SUNY Press.

Kolb, D. A. (1984). *Experiential learning: Experience as the source of learning and development.* Englewood Cliffs, NJ: Prentice-Hall.

Kugelberg, C. (2006). Constructing the deviant other: Mothering and fathering at the workplace. *Gender, Work & Organization*, 13 (2), 152-173.

Kurcinka, M. S. (1998). *Raising your spirited child: A guide for parents whose child is more intense, sensitive, perceptive, persistent, energetic* (2nd ed.). New York, NY: Harper Perennial.

Ladd-Taylor, M. & L. Umansky (Eds.) (1998). *Bad mothers: The politics of blame in twentieth century America.* New York, NY: New York University Press.

Laino, C. (2008). Postpartum depression affects male patients too. *The Medical Post,* 44 (18), 16.

Lakoff, G. & Johnson, M. (1999). *Philosophy in the flesh: The embodied mind and its challenge to western thought.* New York, NY: Basic Books.

Levy, B. (2000). Pedagogy: Incomplete, unrequited. In C. O' Farrell, D. Meadmore, E. McWilliam, & C. Symes (Eds.) *Taught Bodies* (pp. 81-90). New York, NY: Peter Lang Publishing, Inc.

Limbo, R. K. & Rich Wheeler, S. (1987). *When a baby dies: A handbook for healing and helping.* La Crosse, WI: Resolve Through Sharing.

Luther, M. (1915). Defense of all the articles. In C. M. Jacobs (Trans./Ed.) *Works of Martin Luther: With Introductions and Notes* (Vol. II). Philadelphia, PN: A. J. Holman Company.

Lyon-Jenkins, N. (1998). Black women and the meaning of motherhood" In S. Abbey & A. O'Reilly (Eds.), *Re-defining motherhood: Changing identities and patterns* (pp. 201-213). Toronto, ON: Second Story Press.

Man, G. (2001). From Hong Kong to Canada: immigration and the changing family lives of middle-class women from Hong Kong. In B. Fox (Ed.), *Family patterns, gender relations*, (pp. 420-438). Oxford: Oxford University Press.

Mandell, N. & Duffy, A. (2005). *Canadian families: Diversity, conflict and change.* Toronto, ON: Nelson.

Marotta, M. (2008). Relentless rebuke: "Experts" and the scripting of "good" mothers. In J. Nathanson & L. C. Tuley (Eds.) *Mother knows best: Talking back to the "experts"* (pp. 203-212). Toronto, ON: Demeter Press.

Maté, G. & Neufeld, G. (2005). *Hold on to your kids: Why parents need to matter more than peers.* Toronto, ON: Vintage Canada

Mercado-Lopez, L. M. (2008). Con el palote en una mano y el libro en la otra (With a rolling pin in one hand and a book in the other). In A. E. Kinser (Ed.), *Mothering in the Third Wave* (pp. 73-78). Toronto, ON: Demeter Press.

Merriam, S. B. (2008). Adult learning theory for the twenty-first century. *New Directions for Adult and Continuing Education* 119 (3), 93-98.

Mezirow, J. (1990). *Fostering critical reflection in adulthood.* San Francisco, CA: Jossey-Bass

Middleton, W. (2005). Postpartum doulas: Vital members of the maternity care team. In L. Todd (Ed.), *ICEA postnatal educator certification program: Study Modules (I,* pp. 1-3). Minneapolis, MN: ICEA.

Milner, S. (2010). 'Choice' and 'flexibility' in reconciling work and family: towards a convergence in policy discourse on work and family in France and the UK? *Policy & Politics*, 38 (1), 3-21.

Moraga, C. (1997). *Waiting in the wings: Portrait of a queer motherhood.* Ithaca, NY: Firebrand Books.

Moussa, M., & Scapp, R. (1996). The practical theorizing of Michel Foucault: Politics and counter-discourse. *Cultural Critique, 33* (1), 87-112.

Murkoff, H. E., Eisenberg, A. & Hathaway, S. E. (2003). *What to expect: The first year.* New York, NY: Workman Publishing Company, Inc.

Nathanson, J, & Tuley, L.C. (2008). Introduction. In J. Nathanson & L. C. Tuley (Eds.) *Mother knows best: Talking back to the "experts"* (pp. 1-9). Toronto, ON: Demeter Press.

Nelson, A. (2000). Autobiography, imagination and transformative learning. In P. Willis, R. Smith & E. Collins (Eds.), *Being, seeking, telling: Expressive approaches to qualitative adult education research* (pp. 259-269). Flaxton, Queensland: Post Pressed.

Nelson, K. (2010). The small person acquisition project [Radio Series Documentary]. In *The Current.* Toronto, ON: CBC Radio Canada. Retrieved June 21st, 2010 from http://www.cbc.ca/thecurrent/2010/06/june-21-2010.html

Nelson, J., Lott, J. & Glenn, H. S. (2007). *Positive discipline A-Z: 1001 solutions to everyday parenting problems* (3rd ed.). New York, NY: Three Rivers Press.

Nouwen, H. (1990). The *wounded healer* (2nd ed.). New York, NY: Image, Doubleday.

O'Brien Hallstein, D. L. (2008). Second wave silences and third wave intensive mothering. In A. E. Kinser (Ed.), *Mothering in the Third Wave* (ppp. 107-118). Toronto, ON: Demeter Press.

Olssen, M. (1999). *Michel Foucault: Materialism and education.* Westport, CT: Bergin & Garvey.

O'Reilly, A. (2006). *Rocking the cradle: Thoughts on motherhood, feminism and the possibility of empowered mothering.* Toronto, ON: Demeter Press.

Overton, W. F. (2004). A relational and embodied perspective on resolving psychology's antinomies. In J. I. M. Carpendale & U. Muller (Ed.), *Social interaction and the development of knowledge* (p. 19-44). Mahwah, NJ: Lawrence Erlbaum Associates, Inc.

Palmer, P. (2008). *The promise of paradox: A celebration of contradictions in the Christian life.* (3rd ed.). San Francisco, CA: Jossey-Bass.

Penny, L. (2008*). The cruellest month.* London: Headline Publishing Group.

Penny, L. (2008*). The murder stone.* London: Headline Publishing Group.

Piantanida, M., Garman, N. & McMahon, P. (2000). Crafting an arts-based educational research thesis: Issues of tradition and solipsism. In P. Willis, R. Smith & E. Collins (Eds.), *Being, seeking, telling: Expressive approaches to qualitative adult education research* (pp. 94-111). Flaxton, Queensland: Post Pressed.

Pinar, William F. (in press). The primacy of the particular. In Leonard Waks (Ed.) *Leaders in curriculum studies: Intellectual self-portraits.* Rotterdam and Tapei:

Pretat, J. (1994). *Coming to age: The croning years and late-life transformation.* Toronto, ON: Inner City Books.

Pruett, K. (2000). Fatherneed: *Why father care is as essential as mother care for your child.* New York, NY: Broadway Books.

Rabinow, P. (1984). Introduction. In P. Rabinow (Ed.), *The Foucault Reader* (pp. 3-29). New York, NY: Pantheon.

Razack, S. (1998). *Looking white people in the eye: Gender, race, and culture in courtrooms and classrooms.* Toronto, ON: University of Toronto Press.

Reid-Boyd, E. (2005). Mothers at home: Oppressed or oppressors or victims of false dichotomies? In M. Porter, P. Short & A. O'Reilly (Eds.), *Motherhood: Power and oppression* (pp. 195-203). Toronto, ON: Women's Press.

Rich A. (1986). Of woman born: Motherhood as experience and institution (10th anniversary ed.). New York, NY: Norton.

Rich, A. (2001). *Arts of the possible: Essays and conversations.* New York, NY: W. W. Norton & Company.

Rossiter, M. (2002). Narrative and stories in adult teaching and learning. *Eric Digest.* ED473147 retrieved April 30th, 2010.

Sandborn, C. (2007). *Becoming the kind father.* Gabriola Island, BC: New Society Publishers.

Sears, W. & Sears, M. (2001). *The attachment parenting book: A commonsense guide to understanding and nurturing your baby.* Boston, MA: Little, Brown and Company.

Sears, W. & Sears, M. (2003). *The baby book: Everything you need to know about your baby—from birth to age two.* (2nd ed.). New York, NY: Little Brown and Company.

Segura, Denise. (1994). Working at motherhood: Chicana and Mexican immigrant mothers and employment. In E. Nakano Glenn, G. Chang & L. Rennie Forcey *(Eds.), Mothering: Ideology, experience and agency* (pp. 211-233). New York, NY: Routledge.

Shaia, A. & Gaugi, M. (2010). *The hidden power of the gospels: Four paths, one journey.* New York, NY: HarperOne.

Sheedy Kurcinka, M. (1998). *Raising your spirited child.* (2nd ed.). New York, NY: Harper Perennials.

Shorthouse, C. (2009-2010). Communicating with your kids: Tips for now & the years ahead, *Parenting,* Winter, 28-29.

Sinner, A., Leggo, C., Irwin, R. L., Gouzouasis, K.P. & Grauer, K. (2006). Arts-based educational research dissertations: Reviewing the practices of new scholars, *Canadian Journal of Education* 29 (4), 1223-1270.

Smith, D. E. (1987). *The everyday world as problematic: A feminist sociology.* Boston, MA: Northeastern University Press.

Smith, R. (2000). 'It doesn't count because it's subjective!' (Re)conceptualizing the qualitative researcher role as 'validity' embraces subjectivity. In P. Willis, R. Smith & E. Collins (Eds.), *Being, seeking, telling: Expressive approaches to qualitative adult education research* (pp. 132-159). Flaxton, Queensland: Post Pressed.

Soyini-Madison, D. (2003). Performance, personal narratives and the politics of possibility. In N. K. Denzin & Y. S. Lincoln (Eds.), *Turning points in qualitative research: Tying knots in a handkerchief* (pp. 469-486). Walnut Creek, CA: AltaMira Press.

Spock, B. & Needleman, R. (2004). *Dr. Spock's baby and child care* (8th ed.). New York, NY: Pocket Books.

Springgay, S. (2004). *Inside the visible: Youth understanding of body knowledge through touch.* Unpublished Doctoral Dissertation, The University of British Columbia: Vancouver.

Springgay, S., Irwin, R. L. & Wilson Kind, S. (2005). A/r/tography as living inquiry through art and text, *Qualitative Inquiry* 11 (6), 897- 912.

Stadlen, N. (2004). *What mothers do: Especially when it looks like nothing.* London: Piatkus Books Ltd.

Stadtman-Tucker, J. (2008). Mothering in the digital age: Navigating the personal and the political in the virtual sphere. In A. E. Kinser (Ed.), *Mothering in the Third Wave* (pp. 199-212). Toronto, ON: Demeter Press.

Taylor, E. W. & Jarecki, J. (2009). Looking forward by looking back: Reflections on the practice of transformative learning. In J. Mezirow, E. W. Taylor & Associates (Eds.) *Transformative learning in practice: Insights from community, workplace, and higher education* (pp. 275-289). San Francisco, CA: Jossey-Bass.

Thompson, A. (1998). Not the colour purple: Black feminist lessons for educational caring, *Harvard Educational Review*, 68 (4), 522-545.

Timson, J. (2010, July 9). So you expected your kids to make you happy? Get real. *The Globe and Mail*, pp. L1, L3.

Tisdell, E. (2008). Spirituality and adult learning. *New Directions for Adult and Continuing Education* 119 (3), 27-36.

Tuley, L. C. (2008). Half-time parenting: A creative response to Sears and Sears. In J. Nathanson & L. C. Tuley (Eds.) *Mother knows best: Talking back to the "experts"* (pp. 158-164). Toronto, ON: Demeter Press.

Vanier, J. (2001). *Seeing beyond depression.* New York, NY: Mahwah.

van Manen, M. (1990). *Researching lived experience: Human science for an action sensitive pedagogy.* London, ON: The Althouse Press.

Wall, G. & Arnold, S. (2007). How involved is involved fathering? An exploration of the contemporary culture of fatherhood. *Gender & Society*, 21 (4) 508-527.

Wasley, P. A. (1991). *Teachers who lead: The rhetoric of reform and the realities of practice*. New York, NY: Teachers College Press.

West, C. (2009). Truth. In A. Taylor (Ed.) *Examined life: Excursions with contemporary thinkers* (pp. 1-24). New York, NY: The New Press.

Willis, P. (2000). Expressive and arts-based research: Presenting lived experience in qualitative research. In P. Willis, R. Smith & E. Collins (Eds.), *Being, seeking, telling: Expressive approaches to qualitative adult education research* (pp. 35-65). Flaxton, Queensland: Post Pressed.

Wilson, A. L. (1993). The Promise of Situated Cognition. *New Directions for Adult and Continuing Education*, 57, 71-79.

Yates, R. (2000). *Revolutionary road.* (3rd ed.). New York, NY: Random House, Inc.

Zingaro, L. (2007). *Rhetorical identities: Contexts and consequences of self-disclosure for 'bordered' empowerment practitioners.* Unpublished Doctoral Dissertation, University of British Columbia.

Appendices

Appendix 1: Ethics Certificate of Approval

The University of British Columbia
Office of Research Services
Behavioural Research Ethics Board
Suite 102, 6190 Agronomy Road, Vancouver,
B.C. V6T 1Z3

CERTIFICATE OF APPROVAL - MINIMAL RISK

PRINCIPAL INVESTIGATOR:	INSTITUTION DEPARTMENT:	UBC BREB NUMBER:
Shauna Butterwick	UBC/Education/Educational Studies	H09-02144

INSTITUTION(S) WHERE RESEARCH WILL BE CARRIED OUT:	
Institution	Site
N/A	N/A
Other locations where the research will be conducted:	
The research will be conducted at Fiona Lee's home	

CO-INVESTIGATOR(S):
Fiona R.G. Lee

SPONSORING AGENCIES:
N/A

PROJECT TITLE:
learning to be a mother
to be a mother learning
a mother learning to be

CERTIFICATE EXPIRY DATE: June 15, 2011

DOCUMENTS INCLUDED IN THIS APPROVAL:		DATE APPROVED: June 15, 2010	
Document Name		Version	Date
Protocol:			
Proposal for Ethics Review		3	June 2, 2010
Consent Forms:			
Subject Consent Form		3	June 8, 2010
Parent Consent Form		3	June 8, 2010

The application for ethical review and the document(s) listed above have been reviewed and the procedures were found to be acceptable on ethical grounds for research involving human subjects.

129

Appendix 2: Subject Consent Form

THE UNIVERSITY OF BRITISH COLUMBIA

Department of Educational Studies
Mailing address:
2125 Main Mall
Vancouver, B.C. Canada V6T 1Z4

Tel: 604-822-3897
Fax: 604-822-4244
http://www.edst.educ.ubc.ca

Subject Consent Form
learning to be a mother
to be a mother learning
a mother learning to be

Principal Investigator:
Dr. Shauna Butterwick, Associate Professor, Department of Educational Studies (EDST)

Co-Investigator(s):
Fiona Lee, Masters of Arts student in the Faculty of Education, Department of Educational Studies (EDST)

The following persons will have access to this research:
Ms. Fiona Lee, Dr. Shauna Butterwick (principal supervisor), Dr. Carl Leggo (supervisory committee member), Dr. Mona Gleason (supervisory committee member)

Information from this research will be used in an autobiographical thesis written by Ms. Fiona Lee for the purpose of completion of her Master of Arts in Education. The completed thesis will be made available to the library of the University of British Columbia and to the members of Ms. Lee's committee as well as to those persons who have consented to being part of this research.

Purpose:
The purpose of this research is to create an autobiographical map of mother learning and teaching. Your consent is required for details regarding your role in the mother learning of the auto biographer, Ms. Fiona Lee, to be included in this thesis project.

Study Procedures:
In writing stories, reflections, and poetry, Ms. Fiona Lee will create a map of her mother learning and teaching process. Since, as her family member, you have been crucial to this mother learning process references to you will be made in her research and writing.

The research and stories are based exclusively on the experiences of Ms. Fiona Lee and are not taken to be fact or final truth.

This study will not require any of your time.

131

You will be asked to consent to being identified in this thesis after reading an initial draft. If your consent is received, any changes that pertain to you that are made after the fact will require your consent before they will be included in the final thesis document. If you request any changes be made your consent will be required to approve them before the final thesis document is submitted.

Before any portions of this thesis are submitted for publication in a different format you will be consulted and your consent will be requested.

Confidentiality:
Since this autobiography focuses on the author's mothering identity, role, and practice her relationship and interactions with you will be included in a number of her poems and pieces of narrative writing. If at any time you wish to withdraw your permission of inclusion in this autobiography all references to you will be removed.

In order to ensure your confidentiality, during the process of the research, all information will be safe-guarded on the hard-drive of Ms. Lee's computer which is password protected and her written notes or works of art will be securely locked in a filing cabinet in her home office. Only Ms. Lee and her committee members will have access to this research. It will not be made accessible by email or attached to a web site.

Subsequent to the completion of this thesis all relevant computer-generated work will be erased from Ms. Lee's hard-drive and copied to a compact disk (CD) to be stored, along with any hand-written notes, in a locked filing cabinet in Dr. Shauna Butterwick's office at UBC for a period of 5 years.

Remuneration/Compensation:
There will be no fee provided.

Contact for information about the study:
If you have any questions or desire further information with respect to this study, you may contact Dr. Shauna Butterwick.

Contact for concerns about the rights of research subjects:
If you have any concerns about your treatment or rights as a research subject, you may contact the Research Subject Information Line in the UBC Office of Research Services at 604-822-8598 or if long distance e-mail to RSIL@ors.ubc.ca.

Consent:
The inclusion of information about you is entirely voluntary and you may to withdraw your consent at any time.

Your signature below indicates that you have received a copy of this consent form for your own records.

Your signature indicates that you consent to your personal information being included in this thesis.

_____
Subject Signature   Date

_____
Printed Name of the Subject signing above

Appendix 3: Parent Consent Form

THE UNIVERSITY OF BRITISH COLUMBIA

Department of Educational Studies
Mailing address:
2125 Main Mall
Vancouver, B.C. Canada V6T 1Z4

Tel: 604-822-3897
Fax: 604-822-4244
http://www.edst.educ.ubc.ca

Parent Consent Form
learning to be a mother
to be a mother learning
a mother learning to be

Principal Investigator:
Dr. Shauna Butterwick, Associate Professor, Department of Educational Studies (EDST)

Co-Investigator(s):
Fiona Lee, Masters of Arts student in the Faculty of Education, Department of Educational Studies (EDST)

The following persons will have access to this research:
Ms. Fiona Lee, Dr. Shauna Butterwick (principal supervisor), Dr. Carl Leggo (supervisory committee member), Dr. Mona Gleason (supervisory committee member)

Information from this research will be used in an autobiographical thesis written by Ms. Fiona Lee for the purpose of completion of her Master of Arts in Education. The completed thesis will be made available to the library of the University of British Columbia and to the members of Ms. Lee's committee as well as to those persons who have consented to being part of this research.

Purpose:
The purpose of this research is to create an autobiographical map of mother learning and teaching. Your consent is required for details regarding your child's role in the mother learning of the auto biographer, Ms. Fiona Lee, to be included in this thesis project.

Study Procedures:
In writing stories, reflections, and poetry, Ms. Fiona Lee will create a map of her mother learning and teaching process. Since, as her child, your daughter has been crucial to this mother-learning process references to her will be made in Ms. Lee's research and writing.

The research and stories are based exclusively on the experiences of Ms. Fiona Lee and are not taken to be fact or final truth.

This study will not require any of your or time.

134

You will be asked to consent having your child identified in the thesis project after reading an initial draft. If your consent is received, any changes that pertain to your child that are made after the fact will require your consent before they will be included in the final thesis document. If you request any changes be made, your consent will be required to approve them before the final thesis document is submitted.

Before any portions of this thesis are submitted for publication in a different format you will be consulted and your consent will be requested.

Confidentiality:
Since this autobiography focuses on the author's mothering identity, role, and practice her relationship and interactions with your child will be included in a number of her poems and pieces of narrative writing. If at any time you wish to withdraw your permission for your child's inclusion in this autobiography, all references to her will be removed.

In order to ensure your child's confidentiality, during the process of the research, all information will be safe-guarded on the hard-drive of Ms. Lee's computer which is password protected and her written notes or works of art will be securely locked in a filing cabinet in her home office. Only Ms. Lee and her committee members will have access to this research. It will not be made accessible by email or attached to a web site.

Subsequent to the completion of this thesis all relevant computer-generated work will be erased from Ms. Lee's hard-drive and copied to a compact disk (CD) to be stored, along with any hand-written notes, in a locked filing cabinet in Dr. Shauna Butterwick's office at UBC for a period of 5 years.

Remuneration/Compensation:
There will be no fee provided.

Contact for information about the study:
If you have any questions or desire further information with respect to this study, you may contact Dr. Shauna Butterwick.

Contact for concerns about the rights of research subjects:
If you have any concerns about your treatment or rights as a research subject, you may contact the Research Subject Information Line in the UBC Office of Research Services at 604-822-8598 or if long distance e-mail to RSIL@ors.ubc.ca.

Consent:
The inclusion of information about your child is entirely voluntary and you and/or she may withdraw your consent at any time.

Your signature below indicates that you have received a copy of this consent form for your own records.

Please circle one of the below statements to clarify whether or not you consent to having your child be identified in this thesis project:

I consent   I do not consent   to my child's being identified
                                                in this thesis project.

_____
Parent or Guardian Signature   Date

_____
Printed Name of the Parent or Guardian signing above

Printed by
Schaltungsdienst Lange o.H.G., Berlin